The Necklace

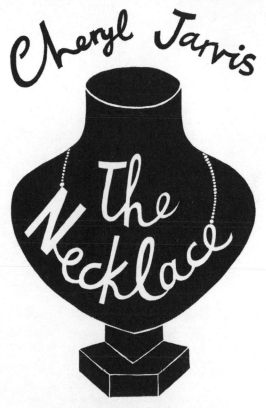

Cheryl Jarvis

The Necklace

A true story of 13 women,
1 diamond necklace
and a fabulous idea

HarperCollins*Publishers*

HarperCollins*Publishers*
77–85 Fulham Palace Road,
Hammersmith, London W6 8JB

www.harpercollins.co.uk

First published in the USA in 2008 by Ballantine Books,
an imprint of the Random House Publishing Group

This edition HarperCollins*Publishers* 2008

1 3 5 7 9 10 8 6 4 2

Cheryl Jarvis asserts the moral right to be
identified as the author of this work

Book design by Barbara M Bachman

Chapter opening photographs © Dina Pielaet

A catalogue record of this book is
available from the British Library

ISBN-13: 978-0-00-727372-0

Printed and bound in Australia by
Griffin Press

For our families and friends
and for women everywhere who imagine possibilities

Here we are, women who have been
the beneficiaries of education, resources,
reproductive choice, travel opportunities,
the Internet, and a longer life expectancy
than women have ever had in history.
What can and will we do?

—Jean Shinoda Bolen

PREFACE

. . .

On SEPTEMBER 18, 2004, THIRTEEN WOMEN IN VEN-
tura, California, went together to buy a diamond necklace.
Within months the media picked up their story. *People* magazine ran a feature. Katie Couric reported on the venture for
the *Today* show. Other segments followed on *Inside Edition,
The Early Show,* and KCBS-TV's *Studio Two* in Los Angeles.
Fox Searchlight Pictures bought the movie rights. Because
the group was in its infancy, the flurry of news stories
barely got beyond the purchase. No one knew then where
the necklace would lead, least of all the thirteen women
who'd bought it.

Here's the whole story, the real story, from the first
sparkle.

CONTENTS

. . .

The Necklace

CHAPTER ONE

Jonell McLain, the visionary

. . .

Making an idea happen

*J*ONELL MCLAIN WAS SITTING AT HER DESK LOOKING AT the piles of paper surrounding her, struggling not to feel overwhelmed. She wondered why she could never clear her desk, never cross off the forty-five tasks on her to-do list. Were there always forty-five things on that list? It sure seemed so. She felt like Sisyphus, the king in the Greek legend who was condemned to push the same rock up a mountain, over and over. Some days she felt like all she accomplished was moving piles. Some papers she could swear she moved a hundred times. Part of the problem was that she was full of ideas, so she was continually adding projects to the list. Executing them, well, that was a skill she hadn't yet mastered.

Today, the list didn't make her queasy as it often did. She'd just finished a deal on a house and so was feeling the high that real estate agents feel when they finally receive their big commission checks. This one represented three months of work and emotional exhaustion. People bought homes when they were undergoing major life transitions, so naturally they were on edge. The shock of prices on the West Coast made those buyers moving to California especially anxious. Because the work was so stressful, Jonell always rewarded herself after each closing.

She hadn't decided what to buy herself this time, so she headed to the mall just to buy her clients a box of See's candy, part of the gift basket she'd have welcoming them to their new home.

The Pacific View Mall was the only mall in Ventura, a California beach town sixty miles north of Los Angeles. Jonell moved her wiry frame quickly through the dusty-pink shopping enclave, stopping only to glance in the window of Van Gundy & Sons, a decades-old, family-owned jewelry store, the Tiffany's of Ventura. Usually Jonell's glances were as quick as her strides, but this time she stopped. She stared.

In the center display case a diamond necklace glittered against black velvet. A few years earlier she'd searched unsuccessfully for a simple rhinestone necklace to wear to a formal event. Now here it was, the exact one she'd had in mind. She recognized the style as the necklace version of the tennis bracelet, so dubbed after tennis champion Chris Evert lost her diamond bracelet during the 1987 U.S. Open and stopped the match to search for it. The diamonds were strung in a single strand all the way to the clasp, the center diamond the largest, the two closest to the clasp the smallest. The gradations were minuscule, the effect breathtaking.

But this was Van Gundy's. There was no way this necklace was made of rhinestones.

Jonell rarely wore good jewelry, though she owned her

share of it—diamond wedding rings from two husbands, 14-karat-gold earrings, pricey watches. Luxury jewelry was something else. Hmm, she thought, wonder what a really expensive piece of jewelry looks like up close? What it would feel like to wear something so lovely and extravagant?

On a whim she entered the store. "Could I see the necklace in the window?" she asked nonchalantly, as if she did this every day.

She reached up to touch the delicate gold chain she wore. Back in 1972 a boyfriend had given her this necklace with the peace symbol pendant, and in 2003, at the start of the war in Iraq, she'd put it on again. She placed the diamond stunner over her old gold charm. It was, she thought, simply exquisite—and exquisitely simple.

She took a breath, and as she breathed out, she asked the price.

"Thirty-seven thousand dollars."

Jonell couldn't stop the gasp. All she could think was *Who buys a thirty-seven-thousand-dollar necklace?*

She looked in the mirror again. She couldn't help but think about the choices she'd made in her life, the ones that guaranteed she could never afford a necklace like this. She thought about how different her life might have been if she'd married a wealthy man or invested herself more in a career. If she'd worked harder, maybe she could have generated the kind of money that would enable her to indulge in this kind of luxury. In the end, none of this mattered, not really. In a world overflowing with need, the idea of owning a thirty-seven-thousand-dollar necklace was morally indefensible to Jonell, who'd mentored disadvantaged kids for six years. Lost in these thoughts, she heard only snippets of the saleswoman's description: 118 diamonds . . . brilliant-cut . . . mined from non-conflict areas . . . 15.24 carats.

Fifteen carats sounded ostentatious and Jonell didn't like ostentation. She appraised it again. There was nothing ostentatious about this necklace. The diamonds were so small, just right for her five-foot-two-inch frame, yet circling clear around her neck they felt substantial. What was magnetic was their radiance. She'd never seen diamonds shimmer like these.

Jonell hesitated to take off the necklace. After admiring it another minute, she laid it back on the counter and thanked the saleswoman for her time.

Over the next three weeks Jonell was surprised how often she thought about the diamond necklace. When she was back at the mall with her eighty-six-year-old mother, Jonell noticed the necklace still in the window. "Mom, I want to show you something," she said, excitedly leading her mother into the store as if she were seven and heading for her first Barbie. "Mom, try it on." Her mother's eyes widened as she clicked the clasp. "It's beautiful," she whispered. Jonell's mother knew quality, so her admiration told Jonell that the design was classic, timeless.

When Jonell peeled her eyes away from the diamonds brightening her mother's neck, she glanced at the tag: twenty-two thousand dollars. On the counter, an ad announced a sale in which the store would take bids on any item of jewelry on display.

Jonell remembered being thirty and in need of a respite. Burned out from her job as a speech therapist in Santa Cruz and weary of her long-term boyfriend, she'd gone to New York City to live with her best friend from senior year at the University of Southern California. Jonell witnessed her roommate washing her face with Perrier. She saw her wrap herself in a full-length lynx coat. That's when Jonell took stock of her own chances for such luxuries. They were slim to nil. That reality aroused not envy but curiosity: Why was personal luxury accessible to so few? After six months, Jonell left New York to return to her native California, but the question had never left her. Now it loomed large again.

Why is it, she wondered, that we can stand shoulder to shoulder to enjoy sumptuous masterpieces in art museums? That whole crowds can admire magnificent landscapes together in national parks? Why can't we share personal luxuries the same way?

And an idea was born: "*I could wear a luxury item if I bought it with other women,*" she thought. "*No one woman needs to have a fifteen-carat diamond necklace all the time. But*"—and here she paused for the clincher—"*wouldn't it be delightful to have one every now and then?*

"*I can't spend twenty-two thousand dollars on myself, but I can spend one thousand. . . . A thousand dollars would not be out of line for most of my friends. . . . If I could convince only eleven women to go in with me, I could bid twelve thousand. . . . It's already come down fifteen thousand. Why not another ten?*"

Jonell started making calls to friends and colleagues. She talked to women in her walking group and investment club. Women she'd met at seminars, parties, charity events.

Most of the women she approached said no. No money. No time. No interest in diamonds. The responses fired off rapidly: *"A formula for disaster. Everyone will fight over it." "What's the point of buying diamonds?" "I can get a better deal at the jewelry mart." "You'll never get twelve women to get along." "If I'm going to spend a thousand dollars, I want something just for myself."*

Even her mother fired off a round: "You'll lose friends over this."

Some comments unsettled Jonell, filling her with self-doubt. Some spurred her to argue. Some she ignored. But she stayed fixed on her goal. She went back to women who'd said no. She asked new women. In two months she had a group of seven. Close enough, she decided. By the time her Visa bill would arrive, she'd have found the rest.

THREE GENERATIONS OF Van Gundy men were in the store the Saturday of the sale: Kent Van Gundy, age eighty, who'd started the business in 1957 and was now retired; Tom Van Gundy, fifty-four, his son, who'd taken over the business; and Sean, twenty-nine, his grandson, who now managed the store.

Tom says he'll never forget that day. Sean won't forget it either. These women were different from the ones the Van Gundys usually encounter. So many women who come into jewelry stores aren't happy, says Sean. Their eyes are anxious, their faces tense. Some are in tears. They're lonely and looking for someone to talk to. Something's missing in their lives, and they're looking to fill the empty spaces. These women rushed into the store smiling, eager to be there shortly after the doors opened to beat any competing bidders. Jonell showed the necklace to the four who came with her, two who'd said yes to her proposition, two who'd said no but didn't want to miss the fun. Mary Karrh, a head taller than Jonell, found herself so far removed from her daily life as an accountant that her expression was one of wonder. If she'd had any fears about what she'd committed her money to, they disappeared when she was face-to-face with the diamond necklace. "Wow, it looks like a million bucks," she said.

"Try it on, Mary," Jonell urged. The other women huddled around Mary, who found herself standing even taller. Her words surprised her: "I can see myself wearing this."

Maggie Hood represented the quintessential California girl with blond hair and a hard body. She moved back and forth, one minute admiring the necklace, the next flirting with a good-looking salesman.

"We need pictures!" said Jonell. One of the women along for the camaraderie ran out into the mall to buy a disposable camera.

Each woman—Jonell, Mary, Maggie, the two friends—posed for a photo with the diamonds. They vamped and giggled, amazed that three of them were even thinking of buying such a thing, even as a "time-share." Obviously these giddy women didn't buy diamonds every day. Throughout the posing, there was awe. "It's so beautiful," they said. They said it over and over. They said it when they saw it on one another and when they looked at themselves in the mirror. They breathed it when Mary wore it with her sleeveless shirt and khaki shorts. They repeated it when Maggie tried it on with her tank top and jeans. And they intoned it as the diamonds lay against Jonell's gold peace symbol charm. "This necklace is so beautiful!" The women swept everyone up in their excitement as they grinned and gushed—and anticipated.

Then it was time for Jonell to hand Tom Van Gundy an envelope. In it was a sheet of legal-sized paper with her handwritten bid and the names of twelve women, four followed by question marks. As she proffered her bid, her posture was confident and her grin playful. But she was nervous. She was asking him to cut his price nearly in half. She was grateful for her real estate experience in negotiating prices, but as she knew all too well from her work, coming in with a low bid might not succeed.

The scene had caught all three Van Gundy men in its footlights. Nothing like this had ever happened in their store. It wasn't just the buzz in the place. In a quarter of a century of working in the business, Tom Van Gundy couldn't recall seeing a single woman buy luxury jewelry for herself. Women fueled the desire, but they waited for the men in their lives to make the purchase.

Tom almost hated to take his eyes off these spirited women to look at their bid, twelve thousand dollars. He winced inwardly. Jewelry stores can have large markups— that's a reason so many chain jewelry stores offer discounts of 70 percent. Being in the jewelry business meant being a negotiator, and in this store Tom usually handled negotiations himself. However, on big-ticket items—and this was definitely a big-ticket item—he needed clearance. This one would be tough to get. Still, he managed to look and sound kind when he said to Jonell, "I need to run some numbers."

He went to the back room. Priscilla Van Gundy, his wife and chief financial officer, was hunched over the books, hyperfocused, trying to tune out the noise. She usually worked in the administrative office across the street, but because of the sale she was squeezed in the store's small stockroom between shelves of inventory and a desk that doubled as a kitchen table.

Priscilla had heard the commotion. She'd figured it was the group of women she'd heard the salespeople talking about, but she hadn't left her desk to see. She avoided looking at customers' faces. She didn't want negotiations to get personal.

"There's a group of women who want a special price on the diamond necklace," Tom said to the thick auburn hair hiding his wife's face. "What can we sell it for?"

Priscilla tapped figures on the adding machine: one for the actual cost of the necklace, another for the number of months it had been in the store, a third for what they needed to make a profit.

"Eighteen thousand," she said.

Tom knew the number wasn't going to fly, but he was used to the back-and-forth of negotiations. He went back to the store front to counter Jonell's bid.

"Not low enough," she said. "We only want to spend a thousand per woman."

Tom had anticipated the answer. He nodded his head and returned to the back room.

"Can we go any lower?" he asked Priscilla.

She felt his apprehension. Thirty-three years of marriage and she could read his emotions like a spreadsheet. She tapped the numbers on the adding machine.

"Seventeen thousand," she answered.

Tom scratched out the twelve-thousand-dollar figure on Jonell's sheet of paper, scribbled fifteen thousand, and showed it to Priscilla.

"Can we do this?" he asked.

"That's ridiculous."

"It could be good for business."

"We sell it for that and we won't have a business."

Tom was silent. Priscilla said more firmly, "That is *not* going to happen."

Tom looked at his wife. He remembered how much more relaxed he'd become after she started working with him six years ago. She had her finger on every dollar, and she was good at it. The business was doing well in large part because of her. More important, he trusted her more than anyone.

But little of that mattered today. Today he wanted her to be flexible.

"I just have a feeling about this," he said to her.

"You sell it for fifteen thousand and we make no profit."

At that moment Tom Van Gundy realized he was willing to let go of any profit. In part, he didn't want to disappoint so many women. It was the same feeling he'd had when he played quarterback in high school and didn't want to disappoint the fans. He knew that turning away twelve woman wouldn't be good business either. Deep down inside, though, he wanted to see Priscilla smile the way these women were smiling, the way he hadn't seen her smile since her sister Doreen had died six months earlier.

Something more important was happening here than making money, something so important that it gave him an idea.

Tom Van Gundy rarely acted without his wife's consent, and he knew if he continued to debate her, he'd lose. Following the dictum that it's better to plead forgiveness afterward than ask permission before, he decided to deal with the repercussions later. He walked out of the back room to hand the number he'd scribbled to Jonell. "I'll give it to you for this price," he said, "but with one condition. I want you to let my wife be in your group." He had no idea how Priscilla would feel about it, if she'd even participate. He just knew he wanted these women in her life.

Jonell looked at the attractive, soft-spoken man in front of her. She couldn't know why he wanted his wife in the group, nor did she know who his wife was or if she'd like her or if any of the women she'd recruited would like her. But the whole idea was about inclusion and sharing, so she didn't hesitate.

"It's a deal," she said.

Jonell wasn't worried about Tom's wife. She was worried that the women she'd worked so doggedly to recruit would balk at paying an extra two hundred dollars. Then what was she going to do? She hid her concern behind her most radiant smile of the day.

Tom returned to the back room.

"I gave it to them for fifteen thousand," he said, again to her bowed head, "but you get to be in the group."

Priscilla looked up at him.

"What are you talking about?"

"The group of women. You get to be part of it."

She knew that he felt bad about the price, so crabby retorts stayed in her head. Had he lost his mind? Had he forgotten that the mall takes 7 percent and the salesman a 3 percent commission? They wouldn't even get their cost out of it. She was always the bulldog, he the golden retriever. Nothing ever changed. What was the point of arguing? It was a done deal.

"Whatever," she said. And that was all she said.

Priscilla stayed in the back room. She had no curiosity about the women. She had no interest in being part of the group. She had no interest in owning a necklace she could have borrowed any time she wanted. All she could think was that if her husband kept making deals like this they'd be out of business. She went back to the books to try to figure out a way to make up for the day's losses.

But Tom Van Gundy saw something his wife didn't. He saw a group of women unlike any others he'd seen in his twenty-seven years of selling to women, talking to women, understanding women. He saw a collective vitality, an unexpected opportunity. He saw *possibility*.

Possibility was what Jonell's vision was all about. It wasn't about a necklace as accessory or art. It wasn't about diamonds as status or investment. It was about a necklace as cultural experiment. A way to bring thirteen venturesome women together to see what would happen. Could the necklace become greater than the sum of its links, thirteen voices stronger than one?

Jonell's confidence wasn't misplaced. By the time her Visa bill arrived three weeks later, she'd lured the final four. Besides a jeweler's disgruntled wife, there were longtime friends, new friends, friends of friends. Their ages ranging between fifty and sixty-two, all but one qualify as baby boomers, that eclectic generation. As a group, they've been married and faithful to one man for thirty-plus years, and they've had three husbands and dozens of lovers. They're childless and mothers of four, with empty nests or kids in Little League. They're dating singles and doting grand-mothers, card-carrying conservatives and lifelong liberals. Some have advanced degrees, others high school diplomas. They've had three careers, checkered careers, one career— in finance and farming, medicine and teaching, business and real estate, media and law. They come from wealth and they're completely self-made. They're Catholic and Jewish, feminist and traditionalist, blond and gray.

No woman said yes to Jonell's proposition because she was interested in jewelry or diamonds. No woman said yes to the necklace because she lusted to wear it. Some wrote a check without even seeing it. Each bought a share because, as Tom intuited, it represented possibility.

What the women didn't know was that over the next three years the necklace would animate their lives in ways they could never have imagined. More important, it would start a conversation. About materialism and conspicuous consumption, ownership and nonattachment. About what it means today to be a woman in her fifties, looking potentially at another thirty to forty years of life. About the connections we make and the legacies we leave, about how to make the most of the long stretch of years.

This is the story of a necklace but it isn't the story of a string of stones. It's the story of thirteen women who transformed a symbol of exclusivity into a symbol of inclusivity and, in the process, remapped the journey through the second half of their lives.

This is a story of transcendence.

CHAPTER TWO

Patti Channer, the shopper

...

Rethinking consuming passions

*J*ONELL SAILED OUT OF VAN GUNDY'S WITH THE DIAMOND
necklace and a quick prayer that the other women would
come through with their checks. But she didn't have time to
worry about that now. She was throwing a party that evening,
and being the last-minute hostess that she was, she still
needed to clean the house and sweep the patio and pick up
the food. But nothing could dull the excitement she felt at
the thought of wearing the diamond necklace. At six o'clock,
she slipped into her black yoga pants and a silk shell the
color of eggplant. Her philosophy of clothes: simple styles,
best of fabrics. She ringed her neck with the diamonds and
stared at the necklace lying against the aubergine shell.

As she continued looking in the mirror, she realized, almost with a start, that the necklace was perfect for her. Her
short blond hair, her rimless glasses, her minimalist
makeup—the necklace looked good with all of it, including
her one concession to glamour, her acrylic nails lacquered
deep red, OPI's Smokin' Havana. She adjusted the arc of the
diamonds to the scoop of her neckline.

No question, she thought, this necklace is amazing. *I
think I'll keep it.*

The feeling of possessiveness vanished as quickly as it

arose, but Jonell was astonished to discover that she had it at all.

The next week, Jonell composed her first e-mail to the women:

"It's about time we got this fabulous group together. We'll meet Thursday, November 11, at four P.M. Please come prepared to talk about the following: the necklace's name, how to divide up the time, insurance, considerations (how we'll refer to rules) and anything else that seems fun, relevant or not. . . . You realize we have created the possibility of being in each other's lives for the rest of the ride. I can't wait to see what happens next."

Priscilla Van Gundy read the e-mail. She'd forgotten all about the necklace and the deal her husband had negotiated, probably repressed it since it was a monetary loss. Jeez, she thought, who's got time for a meeting with a bunch of women? Her reply was terse: "I won't be able to make it. I have to work."

Four miles away, Patti Channer read the same e-mail, relieved to see an agenda. Patti liked structure. She responded immediately: "I'll be there." She laughed out loud. Of course she'd be there. The meeting was at her house.

Well, she pulled it off, Patti thought to herself, remembering their conversation four weeks ago when Jonell had first approached her.

Patti had been driving around downtown Ventura, running errands and listening to NPR's *Talk of the Nation* when her cell phone rang.

"I want to run something by you," Jonell said in her typically excited way.

Jonell was talking faster than the speed limit on Poli Street. Nothing unusual there. What Patti hadn't heard before was Jonell speed-talking about—could it be jewelry? A diamond necklace? Patti pulled over to the curb so she could focus.

"If you and I could do this together and get ten others . . ."

The more Jonell talked, the more confused Patti became. How could Jonell want to spend money on something she'd always considered frivolous? Jonell hadn't even replaced jewelry stolen from her house. She'd met the loss with dismissal: "They were just things." When the two of them went shopping on Montana Avenue in Santa Monica last year, Patti bought a shoulder bag of crochet-wrapped burgundy leather. Jonell was aghast. "How can you spend five hundred dollars on a purse?" she asked.

Patti defended the purchase as a piece of art. Jonell parried that with five hundred dollars she could feed six people for a month. It was easy to understand how the two women had arrived at their different philosophies of spending. Jonell's income from real estate commissions fluctuated, so she had to be careful to plan for the valleys with the money from the peaks. Patti's income from managing her husband's dental practice was steady. Jonell had two children she helped financially. Patti didn't have children, so she didn't have to deny herself. It'd been a running argument between them for the twenty-five years they'd been friends.

That shopping excursion had ended with division: Jonell holed up in a bookstore while Patti dashed off to contemplate the purchase of a chiffon poncho that looked like a butterfly.

Patti's thoughts were yanked back to the conversation by Jonell's command: "You have to go try it on."

"I don't need to. I'm in."

"This could be a really great possibility."

"Fine, I'm in."

"You have to go see it."

"Fine, fine, I'm in," she said for the third time.

Patti didn't need convincing. The idea was so out of character for Jonell that Patti knew it'd be about something else and she knew it'd be interesting. Jonell was the only woman in Ventura who could have tempted her to say, "I'm in." She didn't need to see it.

THE NEXT DAY, Patti stood in front of the window at Van Gundy's. *Yes, it's a gorgeous necklace, I'll give Jonell that,* she thought as she leaned into the display window. *But it's not something I'd buy for myself.* At dinner that evening she talked to Gary about the necklace. Gary was the dashing dentist she'd been married to for thirty-five years. When he sauntered his six-foot-one-inch lanky self into his fortieth high school reunion, the women dubbed him both "best looking" and "best preserved." His brown hair hadn't gained more than a few flecks of gray, and his curls were still thick. After more than three decades together, she knew how Gary, a child of scarcity, would respond:

"How much is it gonna cost?"

"A thousand dollars."

"You're going to share it? That's gonna work?"

"Of course it's gonna work. Women make things work."

"Well, maybe I'll get the guys together and buy a Ferrari."

"You think that's gonna work?"

Gary laughed, and Patti volleyed with her deep raucous laugh.

Gary was skeptical that the "time-share" would work and imagined some kind of *Desperate Housewives* scenario. But he'd found that married life went more smoothly if he didn't interfere with Patti's spending. She earned it, she could do what she wanted with it. Gary chose to look on the bright side: At least now he'd never have to buy her a diamond necklace, thank god.

FOR THE FIRST GATHERING Patti readied her beach house, a cozy, earth-toned duplex decorated with seascapes and shells, with a bedroom loft upstairs and a redwood deck outside. She set out cheeses, French Brie and Irish Dubliner, red and white wines and San Pellegrinos. She chilled a bottle of champagne in her silver wine bucket. She lit the gas fireplace, the white pillar candles on the mantel, and the white votive candles on the coffee table. Patti had a flair for entertaining. This was a meeting, however, not a dinner party, so she'd decided on casual hospitality. She had no idea what was going to happen in her living room. She hoped it wouldn't turn into a free-for-all.

At four o'clock, Jonell strode in with Cokes, and the others clinked in with wine and champagne. Soon the scene replayed the one in Van Gundy's—only with three times as many women, all talking at once. Each took a turn trying on the necklace in front of the mirror, immediately becoming the center of attention as the others crowded around and Patti photographed each woman with her Sony Cyber-shot. Some patted the diamonds like society women in an Edith Wharton novel. Some effervesced like teenagers. Those who'd already tried it on in the store tried it on again, but they did so hurriedly because that wasn't what this meeting was about.

After the ceremonial Trying On of the Necklace, the women squeezed together on the taupe leather sectional and on ottomans and chairs scattered around the small living room. Jonell began the storytelling as if they were gathered around a fire at the beach. She talked about herself, her idea, her excitement, this great group of women. After her narrative, she asked each woman to tell something about herself. She couldn't have known what the other women were thinking as they half-listened, half-analyzed what they were doing in this living room, with these women, and that necklace.

Eleven women—two couldn't make it—all white. Eight blond, two brunette, one gray. Nine with wedding rings, one in heels.

Roz McGrath had been running stats as she looked around the room. *Where are the women of color?* she wondered. *Am I the only brunette here?* She was skeptical of blondes—in her experience she'd found most "blond jokes" too close to the truth. She didn't know most of these women but she wanted them to know who she was. "I'm a feminist" were the first words out of her mouth.

Nancy Huff winced. *The seventies are over,* she thought. *If this is going to turn into some consciousness-raising group I'm outta here*. But she kept quiet. When the last woman finished, Jonell started talking again, about her work, her husband, her kids, what this group was all about. She spoke so rapidly that some of the women had trouble keeping up with her. But her message was clear. "We are not what we wear or what we own," she said. In case they missed the point, Jonell took off her yellow cotton T-shirt, revealing a sheer camisole and an impish smile. Jonell's longtime friends in the group, like Patti, had seen it all before. But what looked to them like an old hippie comfortable in her skin looked different to the newer acquaintances. Some frankly noted Jonell's great body—lean rib cage, firm arms, large breasts—but Roz McGrath was no longer the only one who wondered what she'd gotten herself into.

Next on the agenda: Name the Necklace. Jonell wanted to name the necklace after Julia Child, who'd died two months earlier, on August 13, 2004. The culinary idol had lived her later years in nearby Montecito, where Jonell's husband had built the maple island in her kitchen. Naming the necklace for Child would be a fitting homage to one of the most admirable women of the twentieth century. To Jonell, as well as to the women in the group who'd used her cookbooks and watched her PBS show in the seventies, Julia Child introduced French cooking to Americans with an unpretentious style, an adventuresome spirit, and abundant humor. They appreciated that she didn't come into her own until she was in her fifties, but what they really applauded was her appetite for life. These women saw the spirit of Jonell's homage. Several suggested spelling the name *Jewelia*.

Meanwhile, the rest remained quiet. They thought the idea was ludicrous—the idea of naming a necklace at all, let alone naming it for a cook.

Next on the agenda: the time-share. Each woman would have the necklace for twenty-eight days, during her birthday month. Only two women's birthdates overlapped. Patti's was nine days away, so she was first. Jonell ended the meeting by ceremoniously clasping the diamonds around Patti's neck.

"Don't lose it because it's not insured yet," she said. "And have fun with it."

Patti wore the fifteen-thousand-dollar necklace to bed that night. But she didn't sleep well. She woke up twice feeling panicky. Each time, she touched the necklace to make sure it still circled her neck, that it was in one piece, that nothing was broken. This was the first time since she was thirteen and filched her older sister's gold charm bracelet that she'd worn something that didn't belong just to her. The next morning she felt better, no longer afraid for the safety of the necklace. Still, she fretted over how to put into words what this experience was about. Even if she didn't know exactly what to say, she figured she could look good saying it. She'd select her clothes carefully, choose colors and styles that would complement the diamonds. That'd be the easy part.

PATTI CHANNER GREW UP the youngest of six in Malverne, New York, a small bedroom community on Long Island. Her mother was a fashion aficionado who each season took her daughters on daylong shopping expeditions to the Garment District in Manhattan. First stop: a toss-up between Saks and Bergdorf's. At those tony stores Patti's mother studied the high-end styles. Then she'd take her caravan to Klein's on Fourteenth Street, the Loehmann's of that era. She knew just what to buy. She'd rummage through the piles of discounted designer threads, *zip, zip, zip,* and head back home with the right stuff. Whether by osmosis, training, or something in her DNA, Patti developed an eye for fashion and an instinct for the deal.

By accounts of all four daughters, their mother was a stunner, a stately woman who could wear those designer clothes with élan. She pulled her golden red hair back in a French twist, kept her beautiful nails manicured, and always bejeweled her ears and hands. She was known for her distinctive taste and for dressing her girls in style. She taught Patti and her sisters to take pride in their appearance, and she believed that clothes reveal personality. When Patti started dating, her mother instructed her: "Always look at a man's shoes." When the family moved to the West Coast, Ventura was the thrift capital of Southern California and Patti's mother was Queen of the Thrift Shop. Patti never forgot finding a chandelier for four hundred dollars exactly like one her mother had bought for five dollars.

It's not surprising that Patti's first job while in college was in retail. She worked as a floater for Abraham & Straus on Long Island, and when she was assigned to the jewelry department she bought her first pair of good earrings. They were 14-karat-gold hoops, the size of a silver dollar, the wires intricately bent into a serpentine design.

"They were two hundred dollars—this was in 1970—and I had to put them on layaway. I knew they were one of a kind. They made a statement. When I wore those earrings I felt special. Since that time, I've never gone out of the house without jewelry. Never.

"My love of shopping is genetic, and I consider myself a consummate shopper. I used to pride myself on being able to go into Marshalls and run my fingers over the fabrics and know which jacket was a Dana Buchman. I was never wrong.

"Buying for many people is an aphrodisiac. If they're sad, they go shopping, happy they go shopping, pissed off they go shopping. For me it's the thrill of the hunt, finding the best quality at the best price. I rarely buy retail. I found a beaded gauze top—a work of art—in a thrift shop in Santa Barbara. I paid seventy-five dollars for it. Later when I pulled it out of the closet to wear, I discovered the original price tag—thirteen hundred and fifty dollars. Another find! It felt orgasmic."

Patti didn't feel the same ecstasy with regard to the group necklace. "Diamonds are too common for me. I like artisan jewelry, both because I like unusual designs and because I like to support local artists.

"Besides," she added, "I needed another necklace like I needed a friggin' hole in the head."

IN THE BEDROOM she shares with her husband, Patti talks about her objects of desire, her life as a consumer. It's the perfect setting for the subject. In one corner, a bamboo hat rack is nearly invisible underneath purses—quilted and jeweled and beaded purses, feather and leather, leopard and velvet purses, today's and yesterday's purses. And ohmygosh the boas! Long ones, short ones, they came simple and sequined, in red and chocolate and purple and pumpkin. In another corner, flowing over a wrought-iron quilt stand are wraps and more wraps—silk, woven, textured, fringed. A velvet wrap with mink pom-poms, a black suede wrap with cutout fringe, and a thick felt wrap with oversized pockets. "That one's from Dream Weavers in Martha's Vineyard," she says, "one of my favorite stores." On the bottom shelf of the stand a wicker basket cascades with scarves of cashmere and chenille, painted silks in olive and aubergine. Patti reaches for a gold-and-black-sequined scarf, twists it into a belt, then a headband, then a necklace. "I use a lot of these as costumes," she says. "With the right accessory I can change the look of anything."

No matter what Patti drapes around her lean body, she looks good in it. Her photogenic face is an older version of that of the actress Téa Leoni's. At nearly five feet, seven inches, she has enviable blond hair, thick and wavy, a healthy, outdoor glow, and long limbs seemingly always in motion. Her hazel eyes literally glisten when she smiles— and as Patti gives a tour of her bedroom, she smiles a lot.

More accessories fill the cherry dresser: headbands and sunglasses and reading glasses, all jeweled and tortoise and multicolored and decorated for the holidays. In her walk-in closet: berets in every color, dozens of belts, 150 pairs of shoes. "When I go to Vegas, I don't gamble. I buy shoes," she says. "The boutiques at Caesars Palace have shoes you won't find anywhere else in this country. I don't buy cookie-cutter things. I don't go to chain stores unless I need socks. I like flea markets and thrift stores."

And then there's the jewelry. On one wall, hanging from three etched glass hooks, dangle necklaces galore: chains and beads, rhinestones and pearls, chokers and pendants. In the dresser next to the hooks, she's filled drawers with bracelets and bangles, plus jewelry inherited from her mother and jewelry for every holiday: pins and earrings shaped like wreaths, pumpkins, shamrocks, flags.

And in the closet, a fifty-four-pocket hanging jewelry holder with a pair of earrings in every section; and a thirty-pocket quilted case with jewelry in every section. More necklaces of multiple strands, multiple colors, necklaces made of pearls, gemstones, burros' teeth. "I have a mix of good and fake," she says. "If you have enough good, you can mix in the faux." Patti pulls out a necklace of burgundy silk cording with a tasseled ivory pendant hanging from a burgundy alligator glasses case. She adjusts it around her neck, flips open the glasses case, cocks her head to one side, then broadcasts a huge grin. "Would you look at this?"

The scene recalls the line uttered by the character Clairee, played by Olympia Dukakis in the film version of *Steel Magnolias:* "The only thing that separates us from the animals is our ability to accessorize."

There isn't a drawer, a shelf, a stand, or a chest without hidden stashes and caches of jewelry. The only place Patti doesn't keep it is in a safe.

"After we bought Jewelia a neighbor showed me her diamond necklace, which she keeps locked up. Other women I know make copies of their jewelry and wear the copies. If you're going to do that, what's the point of having it? That first month the necklace was mine to wear, I made the conscious decision that I'd wear it every day."

Patti was off to get her annual Pap smear.

Patti loved her gynecologist. Going for an appointment was never an ordeal, always a fun time. So fun that on one visit Patti talked Dr. Roz Warner into buying a share of the diamond necklace. "I'll join the group," said the doctor, who had recently moved to the area from the East Coast and liked the idea of meeting new people, "but I don't want to buy the necklace."

"Can't do one without the other," said Patti.

The feminine examining room soothed patients, its pale yellow walls decorated with a poster of one of Georgia O'Keeffe's sensual floral paintings. Like many—though never O'Keeffe—Dr. Roz interpreted the art sexually, seeing on the left side of the flower a silhouette of a woman's face and breasts; on the right, her vulva.

In a white cotton gown, the diamonds circling her neck, Patti hoisted herself onto the examining table and positioned her size 7½ feet into the stirrups.

"I have my camera!" she announced.

"No you don't."

"Yes I do. I want a picture."

Patti hadn't been sure how Roz would respond—she was, after all, a physician—so she didn't call her in advance. Patti thought life was more fun if it was spontaneous.

Roz had been in practice twenty years. No one, not one single patient, had ever brought a camera for her annual checkup. She was startled but she moved quickly out to the hallway to nab Michelle, her twenty-five-year-old medical assistant.

Patti prepared the settings and handed the camera to Michelle.

"What do you want me to do with it?" Michelle asked.

"Take my picture."

Michelle looked embarrassed. She knew Patti Channer was one of the livelier women who came through the office, but this was a bit much.

"Just make sure it's a side view."

Patti let rip one of her bar-girl laughs.

Patti's laugh was so infectious that Michelle and Roz laughed too.

Michelle took two shots, returned the camera to Patti, and left the room still laughing.

"Okay, Dr. Roz, now you wear it while you're giving me the exam."

It was an interesting experience, Roz thought, one she decided to repeat when it was her turn with the necklace. It would be a point of conversation, something to distract the patient from the fluorescent lights overhead and the metal speculum inside.

Patti felt good when she left the office. She liked to document her life. Every trip, every family vacation, she was the one with the camera. It was a way of remembering the fun, prolonging the experience. And sharing the photos with people was like giving a gift.

Wearing a diamond necklace for a gynecological exam had to be a first, she thought. She couldn't wait to show the pictures to the women.

—

DURING HER FIRST MONTH with the necklace, Patti wore it
boogie-boarding at a family wedding in Oahu, shooting a
95 on eighteen holes of golf, and helping to hose down a
neighborhood fire. She wore it to her husband's pediatric-
dental practice, where she worked.

And she wore it the orthopedic clinic when Gary under-
went shoulder surgery, and she donned the diamonds every
evening she worried about the fallout from his operation. As
she dragged on her Winston Lights on the patio, she wondered, Would they have to sell the practice? Would she be out
of a job too, after twenty-nine years of running their office,
managing the staff, coordinating the schedules, handling
the books? For a while he'd been the only pediatric dentist in
town, which meant seeing sixty to seventy patients a day.
That had been a lot of work, but gratifying too. She knew that
her business smarts had helped make the practice successful. And Patti had met so many interesting women when they
brought in their kids. That was the way she'd met Jonell.

What if they did have to sell? For the first time in her
life, this turn of events made Patti feel uncertain about the
future. She was sick of people asking her if she was looking
forward to retirement. No, she wasn't looking forward to
doing zilch. She was high-energy, always had been. She
hated that word *retirement*—really, society needed to think
of a new one. Gary was so happy at the prospect, so ready,
but Patti struggled with the unknown that lay ahead, grew
restless just thinking about it. The necklace gave her something else to think about.

Everywhere she went, and Patti went everywhere, she talked about the necklace. Patti was a talker—not a rapid talker like Jonell, but a memorable talker. More than her one-of-a-kind accessories, what distinguishes Patti is her Long Island accent. She left New York in 1975, but the accent didn't leave her. Considering it another accessory, she kept it. When she talks, her hands move constantly, her fingers snapping to make a point, her beautiful, natural nails tap-tap-tapping on the table, the steering wheel, whatever surface is handy. When she walks, she recalls the dynamism of the streets of Manhattan, ever alert, moving quickly, with an athletic stride befitting someone who completed the Waikiki Roughwater Swim. On the streets downtown she talks to everyone—and Patti knows everyone. She calls them "doll," "babe," "honey," "lovey," like a roadside waitress. She tells everyone she bumps into the story of the necklace, all the while accompanied by the percussive cracking of her spearmint Eclipse.

People reacted to the necklace in varied ways. Some marveled, some shrugged, some attacked. *What do you think you're going to do with it?*

Patti didn't have an answer for that one. That comment made her think. *What are we going to do with it?* Scornful comments didn't make her doubt what she'd done; they made her wonder if there was a better way to tell the story. So she changed a detail here, an anecdote there, and she kept talking.

"It surprised me how much fun it was to talk about it. I liked the story of the deal, that is, getting the necklace for the price we did, but mostly I liked the story of the sharing.

I liked that it was another conversation I could have with people. I had no idea where we were going with this, no idea where the necklace was going. Hell, I had no idea where I was going. But I was looking forward to finding out."

PATTI HAD TWO more days with the necklace when one of the women asked to borrow it for a dinner dance. Patti said, "Sure." But when the necklace came back the next day Patti didn't want it. "I'd enjoyed wearing it too much," she says. "I didn't want to become reattached, then have to let it go a second time."

Later with the women, Patti talked about the possessiveness that surprised her, made her feel guilty and embarrassed. Made her feel like Gollum in J. R. R. Tolkien's the *Lord of the Rings* trilogy. Gollum was the character who became mentally tortured and physically wretched from his obsessive desire for the One Ring, "his precious." Patti called the necklace "my pretty." She called her difficulty in letting it go "the Gollum effect."

Collectively buying a necklace was like a real estate time-share, but in that kind of time-share owners didn't get together to talk about their experiences. "In talking about it," says Patti, "I realized that what made the necklace exciting to wear wasn't the necklace itself. If I'd wanted a diamond necklace, I would have bought one a long time ago. What made it exciting was the story behind it. Getting to tell the story was what I'd become attached to."

BEFORE PATTI'S TURN with the necklace would come around again, Jonell, a voracious reader, gave the group a reading list and their first assignment: *Affluenza* by three men no one had heard of. Jonell liked context. "If we're going to talk about the necklace," she enthused, "this book will give us a frame of reference, make us more knowledge-able and effective."

Mary O'Connor, one of the women in the group, was a former English teacher and avid reader of literary fiction. She had no interest in self-help books. *If I'd wanted a book club,* she thought, *I would've joined one.* But she kept quiet. Nancy Huff was quiet, too, while thinking the same thing. In fact, the group's reaction to the reading assignment was like the greeting card headlined "Bad Girls Book Club," where half the group doesn't read the book and the other half doesn't even show up.

Patti wasn't in the habit of reading self-help books either. She liked escapist novels and crime fiction. But since they'd just sold their practice she had time. And she was a member of the Good Girls Book Club; she read the book.

She read that Americans are the most voracious con-sumers on earth, that most of us suffer from owning too much, that everything we own ends up owning us. She read that never before has so much stuff meant so little to so many, and that the relentless pursuit of more will exact a price much steeper than the cost of the goods.

"Reading that book was a turning point," she says. "Until I read it, I never saw myself as a consumer. If I saw a ten-thousand-square-foot home, the excess would not have resonated. How much is enough? was a whole new concept for me.

"For the first time I started thinking about my possessions. When I was younger, I worked at accumulating. If the object I wanted was a 'great deal,' I'd buy two. The book got me thinking for the first time about the excess in my life. I realized that where I've been excessive is with my accessories. I have enough to accessorize every woman in the group. I have at least twenty pair of sunglasses, and how many do I wear? The same pair all the time.

"What I've concluded is that there's nothing I need anymore. I have too much already. I don't wear what I have. Some things I shouldn't have bought in the first place. Like a pair of multicolored lizard high heels. I don't even wear high heels but I had to have those shoes. The urge to buy is like the urge to have a cigarette. It's a need for instant gratification, but if you wait, the urge will go away. We do have a choice. When I was younger I never saw this day coming.

"My mantra used to be 'accessorize, accessorize.' Now it's 'I have enough.' Today when I look in my closet I feel sick. Mortified."

Patti pauses in her self-reflection. "I knew buying the necklace would lead to something unexpected, but I didn't suspect it would change my view of buying. When I was younger I saw what I didn't have and shopped to fill in the holes. Today I see what I do have and shop just to look. Since owning the necklace and having so many conversations about it, I've started to give away my accessories. That's made me feel lighter, made me feel free. If only giving up smoking were as easy."

CHAPTER THREE

Priscilla Van Gundy, the loner

...

Discerning the real jewels

*P*RISCILLA COULDN'T GET EXCITED ABOUT ANYTHING, and that included the first e-mail from Jonell. Scheduling time to spend with a group of women was crazy. She'd always thought so. And now that she and Tom were overhauling store operations she was working sixty hours a week. Who had time? She was beginning to feel like the Bill Murray character in *Groundhog Day,* every morning, even Sundays, waking up to the same life, the same grind. Last year she'd taken off just twelve days, total. The pace had been grueling.

And now one of the store managers had just quit, which meant adding selling to everything else she had to do. Priscilla didn't like being on the floor interacting with customers; she found selling stressful and exhausting—so many women wanting to talk. Occasionally, if the customer was an older man whose wife had recently died, Tom would do the listening. But usually the customer was a woman, and Priscilla was the one to pull up a chair. The same two or three trudged in every week with their slumped shoulders, their sad eyes. They'd talk and talk, sometimes as long as an hour and a half. Then they'd cry. Their husbands had died or left them. Their children were out of town or out of touch.

These women were so lost, their loneliness so palpable. Priscilla knew they were shopping just to fill their days. They didn't want a watch or a ring. They wanted a friend. Priscilla listened and nodded and soothed. Then one day in early December, Priscilla handed one of them a box of tissues to wipe her tears, and in that moment saw the woman as a character out of Dickens, the Ghost of Christmas Future. Would Priscilla be this woman in ten or twenty years?

Sure, today, Priscilla had a job, a husband, three children nearby. But who knew what lay ahead? Wasn't this the lesson she'd learned at her sister's deathbed?

AFTER THE WOMAN LEFT, Priscilla retreated to the back room, where she checked her e-mail.

From: JonellRMcL@aol.com
To: Women of Jewelia

Well, I thought it was really fun, how about you? Mary and Priscilla, we definitely missed you. I think we got a lot done. (Consider this the minutes.)

1. The name Jewelia . . .
2. The schedule . . . to follow from Mary K
3. The considerations, i.e., sharing and not sharing and the promise never to do either without careful thought.
4. Maybe we could do some possibility thinking: Where do you want to take Jewelia? What else could we share? What should everyone share?

I don't know why I took my shirt off. Whose suggestion was that? Someone is supposed to be giving me better advice than that.

We look forward to being together again before Christmas. Further information to follow. You are all fabulous! Have fun.

Jonell

Priscilla stared at her computer. Could she be missing something?

PRISCILLA DE LOS SANTOS ("of the Saints") had grown up in east Ventura, in a predominantly Hispanic farm community. Her Mexican grandparents had settled in Ventura after working as itinerant farmers during the Depression. Her parents started off farming, too, but over time they'd moved on to other work: her mother, packing lemons, cleaning houses, then running a diner; her dad, pouring cement and working construction. The oldest of six, Priscilla spent most of her time at home taking care of her younger siblings. Their family of eight—nine for the five years a cousin lived with them—had to share one bathroom. "So many people were living in that little house," she says. "It was probably one of the reasons I married young—to have my own place."

Her extended family included gang members—too many of them. Her mother was determined her children would not go the way of so many of their cousins. She sacrificed to send them to St. Sebastian, the only kids in the barrio waiting at seven A.M. at the bus stop.

Priscilla grew up surrounded by family, including her grandparents and uncles living across the street, but isolated from her peers. Her remote neighborhood was surrounded by orange groves and mustard fields, the plants tall enough for Priscilla to hide in. "I liked being alone," she says. "But in a way that stopped me from having friends."

She grew up tough. That's what happens when you're surrounded by gangs—and she'd hung around her share of gang types. When she was sixteen, a group of girl hoodlums jumped her and beat her up, leaving red gashes down her arms. "They thought I was a weak little thing from a Catholic school, but I held my own. I've always felt hardcore. It's probably the reason I gravitated to correctional work."

And Priscilla grew up feeling different. When her grandmother descended into dementia, her mother took care of her *abuelita*, which meant Priscilla and her brother had to help run their mom's restaurant. Priscilla was only thirteen.

"I was a really good softball player, but I couldn't participate in sports because I had to work every afternoon and every weekend. I remember a conversation with classmates where we were talking about what we wanted for Christmas. I said I needed a coat. One of the girls said scornfully, 'Why don't you ask for something you want? Why ask for something you need?' But I was lucky to get what I needed. They couldn't understand my world, and I couldn't understand theirs. I thought it'd be the same thing with these women.

"I don't think anyone who grows up like I did ever outgrows the feeling that you're not good enough. I don't think others thought that about me, but I thought it. Intellectually, I knew that friendship wasn't about the way you grew up or the schools you attended, but I didn't feel it. That thinking kept me from reaching out.

"My take on these women was that they'd be upper-crust. I didn't think I was in their league. I felt like I was back in high school. Just thinking about going to a meeting was nerve-racking. Would I fit in? Would I be accepted? What if they didn't like me?"

Priscilla realized she was still staring at the e-mail. She wasn't an e-mail person, hated coming into the office every day to face eighty new messages. All her replies were short. "I'll be there," she typed. "Looking forward to it."

She wasn't looking forward to it. She was just being polite. Being with a crowd of people made her physically uncomfortable. Sometimes she wondered if she had a phobia. Growing up, she always sat in the back of the classroom, anything not to call attention to herself. The extent of her contact with school friends, the few she had, was ten minutes a day.

For most of her life Priscilla had only one close friend—and she lived in Houston. And "close" was a relative term, given that sometimes Priscilla went a year without talking to her. Having one friend sixteen hundred miles away seemed like enough, however, when you worked all the time. And when hadn't Priscilla worked all the time? Ever since she'd greeted, served, bussed, and washed dishes in her mom's diner, she'd worked. She'd borne three children by the time she was twenty-seven and never stopped working.

A crisis with her beloved younger sister hadn't changed that work-work-work pattern. But it caused her to withdraw more deeply into herself. Priscilla's sister, diagnosed with a rare form of cancer, valiantly battled a slow and agonizing death as the disease spread from one vital organ to another. "Doreen was the life of our family, the actress, the jokester," says Priscilla. "With her death I shut down completely. I got up and did what I had to do, but I was just going through the motions. After work each night I'd go straight to the bedroom, put on my pajamas, and climb into bed to watch *American Idol* or *Seinfeld* reruns. I cut myself off from everyone, even my husband.

"One thing I was good at was isolating myself. I'd done it my whole life. It was easier to click on the remote than to reach out to people. But there comes a time when you realize you've spent so much time alone that you've built your entire life around it. And that's not good."

PRISCILLA DECIDED THAT if she was going to this meeting, she was going to make a good impression. Everything in her closet was black, the best color for slimming the extra weight she felt she was carrying. Priscilla had one of those curvaceous and lush bodies that lots of men desire. No matter that real women have curves, Priscilla viewed her body type critically, the result of years of American conditioning.

She chose her best suit, a St. John's knit, and Stuart Weitzman heels. Her jewelry she didn't worry about: on her right hand, a Hearts on Fire diamond ring; on her wrist, a Philip Stein oval dual-time-zone watch, one of Oprah's Christmas picks two years in a row, one the talk show host herself wore. Priscilla had been attracted to the watch because it contained two copper chips, which were supposed to help induce sleep. Since she'd been waking at two every morning and staring at the ceiling, she needed all the help she could get. Priscilla sported the two-thousand-dollar version with a diamond border. One of the perks of owning a jewelry store was that she could borrow whatever she wanted. The downside was that nothing was really hers. If a customer admired her jewelry and wanted to buy it, she took it off that day and never wore it again. It was better to make the money, so she tried not to get attached.

She found a place to park at the historic Pierpont Inn, turned off the engine, and braced herself. Her nerves were frayed. The jittery feeling reminded her of 1994, when she'd wanted to return to college for her degree. For twenty years she'd been raising three kids, juggling temp jobs, part-time jobs, all varieties of jobs from locking down criminals in the county jail to selling cosmetics for Mary Kay. She'd driven to the admissions office, parked the car, turned off the engine, panicked, restarted the engine, drove around the campus, returned to the parking lot, turned off the engine, panicked, restarted the engine, and driven around the campus. Eight times—yes, she'd counted—before she'd finally mustered the courage to go inside to talk to the admissions counselor. Thank goodness she was past that now. No need to circle the grounds eight times.

She was glad she'd paid her share of the necklace. She could've not paid, negotiated that in the deal, but she didn't want to be singled out, didn't want to be different from the others.

By the time Priscilla finished her ruminations and walked into the room, the single chair at the long, rectangular table loudly indicated she was the last to arrive. This wasn't anything new. She was always late to social gatherings. Still, she castigated herself: Being late doesn't make for a good first impression.

Tiny gold lights interspersed in pine greenery gave the elegant, private room at the inn a festive atmosphere. Holly and poinsettias on the fireplace mantel brightened the dark, paneled walls. But Priscilla didn't notice the room. She saw only the women laughing and talking at once. She saw exuberance, camaraderie—the e-mail chatter come alive.

It took less than a minute: She saw what was missing from her life.

"I'm sorry I'm late," said Priscilla, rushing the words. "I had work to take care of."

Before the words sputtered from her mouth, Jonell had jumped out of her seat with a huge smile. She walked quickly over to the newcomer, wrapped an arm around her, and introduced her to the others. Everyone broke out into huge smiles, each woman thinking, *So this is the woman whose generous husband made it all possible.*

Priscilla sat down. She knew it wasn't polite, but she couldn't help staring at the woman across from her. It was Maggie Hood, her straight blond hair and long wispy bangs framing her green eyes, a leopard-print jersey wrapped snugly and suggestively around her muscular body. Priscilla didn't know that women in their fifties could look that good.

Had they had an in-depth conversation, Priscilla would have discovered that the surfaces of their lives were as different as their bodies. Maggie could count three husbands and many friends over the years. But Priscilla had more in common with Maggie than she could ever have imagined just looking at her. Two thousand miles from Ventura, in the inner city of Chicago, Maggie'd grown up tough too.

Maggie smiled warmly at Priscilla, but she felt just as much an outsider. So many women in the group had long-term husbands, while her marriage was spiraling down. So many from the area, while she was a transplant. Although most of the women in the group were mothers, she was the only one still raising kids at home.

Priscilla smiled back at Maggie, then found her eyes drawn to another woman in the group, the woman at the head of the table with the cascading blond hair and the red sweater and the diamond necklace. Priscilla had seen the necklace in the store for over a year but she'd never seen it look the way it looked today. The midday sun, streaming rays of light through the inn's tall windows, magnified the brilliance of the diamonds and cast an aura around the Woman in Red. It wasn't just her face that was suffused with light—it was her whole being. Was it that the necklace needed to be worn to look this beautiful, Priscilla wondered, or was it this time, this place, these women?

Priscilla believed in signs. The first time she'd laid eyes on Tom Van Gundy she saw a light surrounding him, knew in that moment he was the man she was going to marry. The feeling was powerful, spiritual even. She felt something powerful happening here, too. Not as seismic as when she'd been a teenager, this feeling registered more as a tremor, but still, she felt something shift in the ground beneath her: *She wanted to belong.*

Meanwhile, the women were thinking their own thoughts about Priscilla. Every one of them admired her courage in joining a group where she knew no one. A few wondered how this quiet woman would fare with the loud and bawdy characters among them.

When the women were finished with their salads, Jonell passed out an agenda. Number 1: Who's been naughty and/or nice? Hopefully both. Number 2: The cost of the insurance on the necklace: $88.46 per woman. Number 3: How does everyone feel about donating towels for a community project to help the homeless?

The women wrote checks, then got up to leave. They warmly said their good-byes to Priscilla, one by one effusing over how delighted they were to have her in the group. Priscilla caught the contagion of their smiles.

THAT EVENING AT dinner Tom saw Priscilla smile, the first time in a long time, her smile revealing teeth as white as the whites around her warm, brown eyes, now crinkling. He'd fallen in love with that smile when they were in high school, he the starting quarterback, she a cheerleader rooting for him.

"This is a great group of women," Priscilla said. "Thank you for making me a part of the group."

"I didn't do anything."

"Of course you did."

"I just saw those women having so much fun together and I wanted that for you."

"I didn't realize how much I wasn't like that."

"You used to be."

"I don't know what happened."

"I don't know either."

CAN ANY OF US pinpoint the moment when we've lost our younger selves, lost joy in the simple things, stopped celebrating life? For years—decades—we work, raise a family, plant begonias. Then one day we wake up to chemotherapy and eulogies and nursing home visits and the realization that we haven't had a real vacation in years. And all we can do is ask: How did life get so hard?

WHEN JONELL E-MAILED the group the date and place for the next meeting, Priscilla responded immediately: "I'll be there. Looking forward to it." This time she *was* looking forward to it.

But once at the meeting, Priscilla was her reticent, quiet self. She wondered if she'd ever have the confidence to speak as easily and assuredly as so many of the others. In the barrio she'd learned survival skills, not the fine art of conversation. She noticed the women expressed differing opinions, but without raising their voices like the male pundits on Fox News. The women didn't call one another "wrong" or "stupid." Priscilla'd never encountered such civility in dissension. She wondered if the women would be as gracious when she spoke. She did feel the acceptance at the second meeting that she'd felt at the Pierpont Inn— more than acceptance, a sense she was valued, someone special. Her enjoyment in being with the women was beginning to outweigh her fear of not measuring up.

At the fourth meeting Priscilla attended, Jonell ran through the agenda: where the necklace had been, where it was going, what was next for the group. Then Jonell asked, "Anything any of you want to talk about?" Roz McGrath, a veteran of women's groups, was sensitive to those whose voices weren't being heard. "Let's go around the room," she suggested. "Let's give everyone a chance to speak."

Priscilla panicked. She'd have to say something. She couldn't be the only one who was silent. What would she say? One by one the women spoke. As Priscilla listened, she absorbed once again that no one was criticized. Maybe no one would criticize her, either. She started to relax. She uncrossed her arms and legs and breathed. As she thought about what she'd say, she realized she wouldn't speak about issues or news or the necklace. But she would speak.

And then it was her turn. She looked around the room, twelve sets of eyes focused on her. And, odd for her, she found that her need to speak was stronger than her fear of the reaction.

This is what she said:

"Watching my sister die has left my emotions raw and exposed. Everything I feel has risen to the surface. Her death taught me that you have to tell people how you feel about them before it's too late.

"My sister's death wrapped a millstone around my heart. But what I've come to realize is that in dying she also gave me a gift—finding the twelve of you. I am so grateful to be a part of your group. I feel so happy when I'm with you. You have inspired me with your warmth, your acceptance, your joy, the camaraderie you have with one another, the way you embrace life, the way you listen to one another without criticism, the way you have welcomed me into your lives. I know now the meaning of the word *inspire*. It means 'to breathe.' You have breathed life into me. Thank you."

As she spoke, Priscilla's eyes had filled with tears. By the time she'd finished, the other women's had, too.

PRISCILLA'S FIRST TIME with the diamond necklace, she wore it to the office, to the grocery store, to the bank, to a seminar. She didn't pick special clothes to flaunt it, didn't talk about it. She knew she should put more time into wearing jewelry. For one thing, wearing jewelry couldn't help but be good PR for the store. But Priscilla wasn't a jewelry kind of woman. When she and Tom traveled to trade shows, she noticed other women decked out in big rocks. Flaunting the inventory didn't interest Priscilla. She enjoyed looking at bling on other women, but she didn't need the billboard for herself. Adornment was the last thing she thought of when getting dressed. Not a great thing for a jeweler's wife to admit, but the desire just wasn't there.

The desire wasn't there for the diamond necklace, either. Wearing it meant *nada*. What excited Priscilla was thinking about the next meeting, the one where she'd cede the necklace, the night she'd get to be with the women again, the night the gathering would be at her house.

Six weeks ahead of time, Priscilla started planning and preparing. She ironed her white linen tablecloth and matching napkins. She polished her silverware and serving trays. She brought out her Wedgwood "Columbia" china and cranberry-colored crystal stemware. She ordered a feast from the Wood Ranch BBQ & Grill in Camarillo: cold shrimp and finger sandwiches, barbecued shredded beef, assorted salads and breads. She baked a rocky road fudge cake, what had once been her signature dessert but which she hadn't made in seven years. The final touch: Chambord and champagne. She knew several of the women loved champagne, so she reached for the bottle of Dom Perignon that someone had given the Van Gundys as a Christmas gift three years earlier. There had been no special occasion since then, no reason to open it.

Priscilla grimaced at the yellow stain her daughter's Maltese puppy had showered on her cream-colored carpeting, but she knew the women wouldn't notice. Why should she care? The food looked wonderful, but even that wasn't important. These women were casual hostesses. They wouldn't care what she served.

Five minutes before six, she opened the double doors of her two-story brick-and-stucco home and stood outside waiting. Geraniums lining the walkway were blooming, a burst of fuchsia and rose.

As was their custom, the women arrived in groups, everyone talking and laughing as they strode through the door. Serenely welcoming them: Priscilla in the doorway and behind her, a five-foot statue of the Virgin Mary, tucked into an entryway alcove, the sky painted in trompe l'oeil.

The women smiled and hugged with exclamations of "Love your hair," "How was your trip?" "Oh wow, look at the food." After the outpouring of goodwill, everyone gravitated to the dining room table. Several headed straight for the champagne. Brows lifted or jaws dropped when the women alighted on the Dom Perignon.

"Do you have any idea what this is?" Dale Muegenburg asked Priscilla.

"I'm not familiar with it, but I think it's expensive."

"It's about five hundred dollars a bottle."

"I had no idea."

"Now that you know, you sure you want to open it?"

"I'm sure. This is a celebration."

Before the meeting got under way, the champagne lovers agreed: best bubbly they'd ever tasted.

"BEFORE MEETING THESE WOMEN," says Priscilla, "I was always fending things off, always saying no. In the store Tom would ask me for a lower price, like he did with the diamond necklace, and I'd say no. He's ask me if I wanted to go on a trip to Hawaii, I'd say, 'We can't afford it.' When my daughter went on trips with her girlfriends I'd give her a hard time. She works in the store and I thought she shouldn't be doing something frivolous. I sucked the life out of everyone around me.

"My life was family and work for a very long time. And everything revolved around work. I knew it wasn't the most important thing but I acted as if it were. Work became a habit, and it was enough.

"But I wasn't prepared for how much life would change. Since the death of my sister and this year, my father, my family isn't the same. My kids are adults now with their own families. That's not the same, either. When they were growing up I was the disciplinarian. Now that they're on their own I don't want to say anything that will upset them. I'm close to my kids, but there's always a sense of needing to be careful, not overstep my bounds, especially with my daughters-in-law. You have to know when to speak up, when to retreat. Mostly retreat. It doesn't matter how good your ideas, how careful your words, adult children hear suggestions as criticism. So I won't even make suggestions anymore—it's my most difficult task. And then as a businessperson, you have to make sure you say the right thing to the right people. There's a consciousness and a cautiousness to every conversation.

"With these women I can let all that go. The day I know I'm going to a meeting that night, the work goes faster, easier. I move with a lighter step. Now I'm always asking, 'When's the next meeting?' I had so much fun the night I hosted the group. That was the first time I'd entertained in years, and the first time in my life I wasn't nervous about having guests. I didn't want the women to leave. Sharing myself and my home with them made me feel peaceful, made me feel complete.

"Going to the meetings was the beginning of my saying 'yes.' 'Yes' to showing up. 'Yes' to reaching out.

"Negotiating my being in the group was the greatest gift my husband ever gave me. He gave me my life back. He gave me a future."

CHAPTER FOUR

Dale Muegenburg, the traditionalist

. . .

Rekindling the marital spark

D . . .

ALE MUEGENBURG WOULDN'T GET TO WEAR THE necklace for eleven months. She hated to wait that long. Wouldn't it be fun to wear it to her dance club's annual "away" dance in San Diego? She called Roz McGrath.

"Sure, you can borrow it," Roz said when Dale called her, "but I won't be home. I'll leave it for you on the front porch." Imagining a typical neighborhood house, Dale shuddered. Outside where anyone could see it? Unguarded? What was this woman thinking? The necklace wasn't insured yet. What if someone took it? Would Dale have to come up with the money to replace it?

Dale tensed as she packed the last few items in her overnight bag, and she stayed tense during the drive to Camarillo, fifteen miles south of Ventura. She urged her husband, Ted, to drive quickly. She didn't relax until after Ted had maneuvered a long, winding gravel road, atop which sat Roz's isolated farmhouse.

Dale raced to the front door to grab the silver jewelry case, then clutched it on her lap for the three-hour drive to San Diego.

Now a new kind of uneasiness crept into her thoughts.

Would people think the necklace was a fake? With jewelry, Dale subscribed to the "less is more" philosophy. As a real piece of jewelry the necklace was elegant, but as costume jewelry it'd be garish. On the other hand, a real diamond necklace oozed status. And status symbols made Dale squirm. Like many women, she was susceptible to their allure—a Rolex watch was the only gift from her first husband that she'd kept. Yet she felt shallow when she succumbed. She loathed showing off. How embarrassing if people thought she'd bought a status symbol. Now guilt agitated the emotions swirling through her like images in a kaleidoscope.

Why did putting on this necklace feel like such a momentous act?

At the Rancho Bernardo Inn, Dale shed her sandals for heels and her denims for a sleeveless, black crepe cocktail dress. She carefully took the necklace from the case to clasp it around the nape of her neck. As she looked in the mirror, emotions swelled and swirled again. At first, she felt elegant, regal, like Princess Grace. A moment later, her composure crumbled. Why did seeing herself wearing the diamonds disturb so? How was this possible? She'd longed to be a part of this experiment. She'd struggled just to join.

DALE MUEGENBURG WALKED regularly with Jonell and Nancy Huff. Three times a week, the three of them met at seven-thirty A.M. at Palermo, a coffee shop downtown on Main Street. The women walked west on Main, past the Mission toward Ventura's pier. They breathed in the salt air from the Pacific and finished up an hour later with cheese bagels and double lattes. Dale had been one of the first to hear Jonell's idea and one of the first asked to participate.

The idea appealed to Dale but not the expense. Money was an issue. Dale hadn't worked full-time since she'd been a paralegal at Ted's law firm, where the two of them had met twenty-seven years ago. With her marriage to Ted, a widowed attorney with three children, Dale felt she'd acquired a full-time job at home. She'd tried various part-time gigs, including two years as a high school French teacher. But five years ago, Ted's elderly mother needed care, so Dale had withdrawn from the workforce completely. Which meant she didn't have an independent income. Which meant she could spend a hundred dollars without consulting her husband, but not a thousand.

At dinner that night, she didn't mention the necklace because she was nervous about telling Ted. She needed time to figure out the best way to approach him. She wasn't going to ask his permission, but she wanted his support.

Go slowly, she told herself, get a sense of his feelings about it. Just put the idea out there, let it simmer.

Ted was a good listener—a trait that contributed to his considerable charm. He seemed to take in every word he heard, and even more, he seemed genuinely interested in what people had to say. He was five feet, nine inches, bald and bespectacled, and exuded sex appeal.

So the night Dale told Ted about the necklace-sharing plan, Ted focused on what Dale was saying. His face said, "Tell me more," but his mind asked, *Was I hearing her right?*

The three walkers were going to buy a twenty-two-thousand-dollar necklace? Was she crazy? If these were the kinds of women she walked with, she needed a new group.

Aloud he said noncommittally, "You girls."

Two weeks later, Dale brought up the subject again.

"Jonell's idea looks like a go," she said. "I'd like to be part of it."

Not this again, Ted thought. "You already have nice jewelry," he said.

"This is more about sharing it."

"I didn't think you liked diamonds."

"There may be more to it than wearing it."

I am not on board with this. "I still don't get it."

When Dale met resistance she didn't push back. That characteristic had served her well when she was twenty-nine and the "overnight" mother of teenagers. And it'd served her well in her marriage to Ted. She dropped the subject.

While Dale was calculating how best to win over her husband to the purchase, her husband was calculating how best to talk her out of it. He hadn't been in the legal profession for three decades without becoming a strategist, too. He knew he couldn't—wouldn't—stop her, but who knows what resentment he'd harbor? And resentment, he knew, could damage a marriage. But they were still paying pricey college tuition for their youngest daughter. At this point, a diamond necklace was an extravagant and unnecessary bauble. More than questioning the expense, though, he realized he was hurt. He'd given Dale so many beautiful pieces of jewelry in their twenty-four-year marriage. Weren't they enough? And why would she want diamonds? Flashy wasn't her style. She was understated, tailored.

Ted decided to talk to Wayne Huff, whose wife, Nancy, had agreed to the venture. Wayne was a general contractor with a gentle manner and a warm smile.

"I think this is a bad idea," Ted said one Sunday afternoon at Wayne's house.

"Why?" asked Wayne. "It means a lot to the girls. You'll be happier if you let her do it."

"Why do you think that?"

"You think you'll be happy with an unhappy wife?"

"No. . . . But the expense . . ."

"Think of it as an investment in your relationship."

Ted liked and respected Wayne, so his words carried weight. Intellectually, Ted knew Wayne made sense. But emotionally? Ted still wasn't sold on the idea.

And Dale knew it. On her next walk with Jonell, she confided her anxiety about finding a way to overcome Ted's resistance.

How to get the husbands enthusiastic? Ideas were Jonell's forte. This one she figured out early on. She'd had to when few husbands responded like Tom Van Gundy to their wives buying a diamond necklace, even sharing the purchase. Jonell's husband had thought the idea was absurd. So did a number of others. They'd rolled their eyes, they'd teased, they'd smirked. Their reactions, whether strong or subtle, relayed the message: *Man, what a frivolous idea.*

The obvious tactic to change the male mind-set, Jonell decided, was sex.

"We'll have a rule," she said, her eyes full of mischief. Jonell's eyes were usually full of mischief. "Well, not a rule, because I don't believe in rules. We'll have a guideline. Each woman, when it's her time with the necklace, has to make love wearing only the diamonds."

She paused, then smiled her impish smile. "Why can't women take over the world with sex and diamonds?"

Dale didn't know if the ploy would work, but she wasted no time giving it a shot. At dinner that night, she mentioned the "guideline," treating it as a joke to cover her embarrassment. She was discomfited by the ruse, even more by the vision of herself naked with the necklace.

Jewelry as a pleasurable sex-inducing object? Ted had never imagined such a thing. But the image immediately seduced him. *What a way to dress up my wife's gorgeous body.*

He smiled. "You definitely have to do this."

With that, Dale cleared the last hurdle with the ease of a Florence Griffith-Joyner.

NOW HERE DALE WAS in her hotel room wearing the necklace for the first time.

The moment of feeling like a royal had vanished. Now she was feeling more like a chambermaid. *My dress isn't worthy of it.* From there it was a short step to *I'm not worthy of it. I'm too heavy.* Looking in the mirror at the beautiful necklace and her size 14 dress, Dale realized how tired she was of not feeling good about herself. In front of the mirror, she made a vow: I will lose twenty-five pounds. When the necklace is mine to wear eleven months from now, I'll shimmy into a size 8.

—

REMINISCING ABOUT THAT moment in front of the mirror, Dale says, "Part of not feeling good about myself was that I didn't care about sex anymore. I'd always seen myself as someone with a strong sex drive but with menopause it just ended.

"In the beginning of our marriage the sex was really good. Then over the years things changed. I got pregnant, out of shape, gained weight, didn't feel sexy. Kids were coming and going. I was distracted, tired. Life got in the way.

"Sex began to feel like childbirth. You remember that childbirth was painful, but over the years you forget just how much it hurt. I knew that I used to love sex, but I couldn't remember what desire and enthusiasm felt like.

"A lot of women in their fifties don't care about sex anymore. I've talked to a number of married women who haven't had sex in years. People get into ruts, then they become comfortable there. It's easy to see how it happens, but women put themselves at risk for their husbands having affairs. For me that'd be devastating. I made a conscious decision that I'd become interested again.

"I heard a doctor on a talk show say that the 'more sex you have, the more you want.' He recommended a book called *The Sex Diet.* The only copy I could locate was a used one, online at Powell's. When I told a friend, she said 'Eww, a used copy of a sex manual.' I hadn't thought of that, so I was relieved when it arrived in its original, sealed wrapper. The book came with little booklets, one for him, one for her, full of ideas. I gave it to Ted for Valentine's Day as a joke. Neither of us read the book, but I glanced at the tear-out booklet. I was too shy to do anything extreme, but the ideas stirred my imagination, got me wondering what I could do to be more lively and enthusiastic.

"Then I signed up for a seminar on intimacy. It wasn't a couples seminar per se but we both went. It made a much bigger impact than I'd ever anticipated. We both realized we weren't communicating. In fact, for more than twenty years we'd never talked about sex. Only some oblique references if I was saying 'no' too much, and that was hardly a conversation. I was shy about initiating sex, and talking about it felt embarrassing to both of us.

"After the seminar, we came up with a code, a playful phrase to gauge each other's gameness for sex. It was a way to signal each other without being too explicit. We've more or less abandoned it because we're more open and straight-forward now, but having this way of communicating was groundbreaking for us.

"Losing weight made a big difference. In eight months' time, I lost those twenty-five pounds I'd vowed to lose. Ted didn't mind when I was heavier, but losing the weight made me feel sexier.

"The biggest factor was finding an endocrinologist and telling her my sex life could be better. She put me on hormones and testosterone. The side effect has been a little more hair growth on my face—I'm continually plucking—but it's worth it. The testosterone launched me into a whole new realm.

"Now I'm the one who wants sex more often. And I've become a lot less inhibited. Here's an example. When we were getting ready to go to Ted's college reunion we signed up to stay in the dorms. He's eleven years older than I am, so he was in school before the sexual revolution. I started thinking about that time from his perspective, that he probably would have liked to have had a girl in his room. Playing into what I imagined his fantasy would be, I ordered a schoolgirl outfit: a plaid, pleated miniskirt, a sexy white blouse, and kneesocks. I knew I'd be embarrassed to buy it in an adult store in Ventura, so I ordered it by mail. If I'd tried on the outfit in a store I wouldn't have bought it. Pleats don't do a lot for me. The dorms had communal bathrooms, so to surprise Ted I had to put the outfit on in the bathroom, then cover up with my bathrobe. I didn't want anyone else to see me in this getup. It was fun, and Ted seemed to appreciate it.

"I'm getting less embarrassed all the time about trying new things. It's fun to look online at all the paraphernalia and costumes—cowgirls, harem girls, bar wenches. I wanted to try watching erotica, so I went online for that, too. I thought the movies were fun and stimulating, though I always wanted more of the story, while Ted, typically male, wanted to fast-forward to the sex. I'm continually thinking, 'I wonder if this would be fun to try.'

"Making love with the diamond necklace was definitely fun, and sexy. We were giggling. It lent glamour and drama to the experience. I felt like I was on a movie set.

"At first when I was becoming more experimental I worried that I'd shock Ted. He came from a more conventional era. I didn't want him to lose respect for me, think I was acting slutty, so I ventured cautiously. But he was fine with everything I tried, actually more than fine. The more appreciative he was, the more relaxed and confident I became. All of a sudden I wondered why I was being so coy."

DALE HAD NOT GROWN up with coy women. The oldest of three girls, Dale was raised in an upper-middle-class family in Palo Alto, three houses away from the Hewletts of Hewlett-Packard fame. That neighborhood didn't leave the deepest impression on Dale. The women in her childhood did that.

There was her exotic aunt Jeanne, who worked for the foreign service. She filled Dale's home with artifacts from her posts: gazelle sculptures and zebra drums from Nairobi, a camel saddle and bust of Nefertiti from Cairo. She brought Dale a kimono from Hong Kong, a red leather jewelry box inlaid with silver hieroglyphics from Egypt. With her animated storytelling, she opened Dale's mind to the fascinations of other cultures.

There was Dale's mother, Mary, a "Rules" girl before *The Rules* was published. She taught Dale that if a boy was fifteen minutes late picking her up, she should refuse to go out with him. Dale wasn't sure about such rules, but she could see that they worked for her mother, who'd attracted three marriage proposals before saying yes to Dale's father. During her years as a young widow, family photograph albums showed Mary on the arms of a succession of handsome boyfriends. She didn't have to work at attracting male attention, but she was comfortable receiving it, at ease in her sexuality. When her daughter boldly asked about her sex life with their father, Mary said, just as straightforwardly, "It's great." Greeting cards sent to her mother on her eightieth birthday reminded Dale of her mother's success with men. One called her "sexy Mary"; another, "neighborhood bombshell." In her retirement home, three men were vying for her attention, calling daily and bringing gifts.

And then there was Dale's grandmother, Neva. She was an elegant woman who always kept long-stemmed red roses on her coffee table, but she was also a colorful character. While Dale was at the University of California at Santa Barbara, eighty-year-old Neva was enjoying a much younger boyfriend, who was a pilot. "We have a wonderful physical relationship, too," she'd say to Dale with a wink and a smile. Neva taped affirmations to her mirror and encouraged Dale to read books on positive thinking.

After someone ran naked across the stage at the 1974 Academy Awards and "streaking" became a fad, especially on college campuses, Dale's family was gathered one evening when Neva, who was visiting, ran through the living room stark naked. She'd shocked the whole clan. After putting her clothes back on, she joined the family on the sofa and everyone convulsed with laughter. As a teenager, Dale felt a little embarrassed by her grandmother's antics. But even then she could see what an alive and happy woman she was.

"SO THE WOMEN IN my family enjoyed sex," Dale reflects, "which was good for me. It made sex feel normal and natural and healthy.

"Still, it can be hard for long-married women to sustain the interest in sex, the energy and the excitement. It's important for women to push themselves, because for men to feel loved they need sex. Visual stimuli evoke an automatic response from men, so it's harder for them to suppress their sex drive. For women sex is more mental. We have to create a fantasy in our minds. But that means we have more control over our sex drives, which is good for women. It means we can change our mentality. We can rev up our sex life.

"I probably could have revived ours sooner if I'd known then what I know now. You have to make it a priority."

IN THE MUEGENBURGS' comfortable, art-filled Ventura home, Dale's kitchen reveals two loves: gourmet cooking and French culture. Seven shelves of cookbooks encase titles ranging from *Food Lover's Guide to Paris* and *At Home in Provence* to classic tomes by Julia Child and Jacques Pépin. Acrylic file boxes store five years' worth of back issues of *Gourmet* and *Bon Appétit.* Colorful French pottery sits on the taupe tiled countertop. Mauviel copper pots hail from E. Dehillerin, the Paris restaurant-supply house that Child frequented. A framed menu from Taillevent, a grande dame of Parisian dining, hangs on one wall.

Dale's making eggplant parmesan for dinner. She converses easily as she cooks.

"What I like so much about French culture," she says, "is the way the people take time to enjoy life. They savor fine food, fine wine, sex, conversation, almost developing them into art forms. The French don't live to work. I'm at a place where I could work full-time again, but getting only one or two weeks off a year is no way to live."

Dale is the sole woman in the group not working outside

the house. She exploits much of her leisure time to savor life as the French do, to entertain couples with gourmet feasts, to remember friends' birthdays with carefully selected cards and gifts, to pamper family with prolonged birthday and holiday celebrations.

But staying home in our career-obsessed society, she's discovered, exacts a price. " 'What do you do?' is a hard question to answer. Some people immediately lose interest in you. An investment club and charity work don't seem to be enough. You have to account for yourself in an interesting way. Jewelia has given me something interesting to talk about."

Dale's wearing cotton slacks and matching collared shirt in a midnight-blue-and-black pattern of tiny checks, the shirt unbuttoned to reveal a black lace camisole. Her clothes hang loosely, the result of a recent holistic diet. From her highlighted hair to her pedicured feet, her look is polished and pulled together. You can see her walking along the Champs-Élysées, looking much more like a Parisienne than a tourist. Her voice is Kathleen Turner husky, her face unlined but also unpulled by plastic surgery. "I'm philosophically opposed to doing anything drastic," she says, "but if there's a lotion or hormone that'll help, I'll go for it." She recently started using Obagi's skin care line. Her skin glows.

As Dale cuts the eggplant into half-inch-thick slices, Ted walks in, his step signaling his buoyant mood. Six A.M. at the boxing gym, a productive day at his firm where he specializes in estate planning, and now home, where's he greeted by the aroma of tomato sauce simmering with onion and garlic and basil. His clothes hang loosely, too.

"Dale's the cook," he says. "I'm the maître d', the sommelier, and the cleanup crew."

As Dale sautés the eggplant in peanut oil, Ted narrates the story of one of his serving faux pas. Dale had volunteered to cook a beef tenderloin for an al fresco gathering with another couple. She'd stored the cream sauce in the same type of foil-covered container that she used for leftover cat food. Assigned to pack the picnic basket, Ted grabbed the Friskies instead of the *sauce moutarde*.

"I took it pretty well," says Dale, "at least in my memory."

"When have you ever made a scene?" asks Ted. "I don't believe you have."

"A spectacle perhaps."

He looks at her and smiles. "Yes, those have been fun."

The conversation segues to the first month that Dale had Jewelia. The couple had decided to go to Paris, a favorite vacation spot, to celebrate Dale's birthday and to visit their youngest daughter, who was working as a paralegal at the Paris office of a New York law firm.

Dale always looked forward to trips, but on this one she'd be wearing Jewelia. The second guideline, devised by Jonell, was that if any of the women went to Paris, she could take the necklace, in honor of her namesake. Dale thrilled to being the first woman in the group to honor both guidelines. And no question, wearing the necklace with a size 8 outfit was more fun than wearing it with a 14. She loved the way the diamonds lay on her neck more attractively now, shaped more like a V than a U.

Ted, a natural raconteur, picks up the story line. The two of them had developed a rhythm for travel, he explains.

Dale, a researcher extraordinaire, planned the flights, hotels, and restaurants. She studied the local history and culture. Conversant in four languages, she brushed up on the native tongue. Ted planned the activities.

"I knew just what I wanted to do," Ted says. "Show Jewelia Paris. See the city through the eyes of a newcomer."

"Can you make the salad while you talk?" Dale asks him.

As Ted continues the story he washes leaves of romaine, slices a red onion, thinly peels an avocado. Like Dale, he works easily while he chats.

"We climbed with Jewelia to the top of the Eiffel Tower. We took her to the Louvre. To walk along the Seine. To see l'Arc de Triomphe and la Musée d'Orsay. And we took her to Cartier—that was probably the highlight. It was my idea to introduce Jewelia to a French cousin or great-aunt. Take her picture with a wealthy relative." His tone of voice reflected amusement as if Jewelia were a member of the family.

The couple was feeling a little intimidated as they approached the luxe surroundings: the classic awning heralding one of the world's most exclusive stores, the jacketed doorman, the posh gilded display cases, the tall willowy blonde who approached them. Cartier has a strict policy, she told the Muegenburgs: no photographs in the store. But when she saw the couple's visible disappointment, she whispered, "Follow me." Leading them to a freestanding display case in a corner, she said she'd make an exception for their "leetle tennis necklace." Ted photographed Dale and Jewelia beside a resplendent triple-stranded, diamond necklace.

"Not a cousin," Ted decided, "more like Jewelia's great-grandmother, the baroness."

"And then we took her to the cathedral of Notre Dame, because Jewelia sleeps around. She needed to make her confession, so what better place? Tom Van Gundy can clean her but that's only surface work. We sat in a pew and thought for a while about her sins. I really think she had a bit more luster when she came out."

"Dinner's ready," says Dale.

Ted sits down, takes a bite of his eggplant, then looks appreciatively at his wife.

"This is really good." He smiles at her.

"You have dimples," she says, a reference to a result of his weight loss. She puts a hand on his arm. "They're so cute."

He smiles sheepishly. "You're embarrassing me."

Ted concludes his story: "Looking at the city as if it were our first time, we noticed details that gave the experience new texture and expression. It was a different kind of trip and it was a blast—one of the most fun trips we've ever had."

AND SO, THE HUSBAND most resistant to his wife's buying a diamond necklace is perhaps the husband whose life has been most enhanced by it.

"A few years ago, when my mother died and our youngest daughter left home, our active caretaking came to an end," says Ted. "Now the two of us romp around the house.

"In many ways Jewelia is emblematic of both of us liking ourselves better. Part of it has to do with body image. I've lost forty-seven pounds, some of it from chasing Dale in the necklace so we could honor the guideline. My weight loss interrelates with hers. We're terribly codependent, so we encourage each other's habits.

"And part of it is that Dale's become more self-confident. And that's been a huge benefit for me. Sometimes I forget how old I am. In my wildest teenage years, or even ten to fifteen years ago, I could not have imagined a sex life like I have today. It's incredible. And I don't take anything for it, either.

"Through Jewelia I've learned the value in letting go of control, being willing to let something take on a life of its own."

CHAPTER FIVE

Maggie Hood, the adventurer

...

Striving for a healthy life

*L*ISTENING TO THE OTHER WOMEN'S ADVENTURES WITH the necklace was painful for Maggie Hood. She was probably a bigger adventurer than any of them. She'd bungee jumped in New Zealand, camped in the Australian outback, cycled the Pacific Coast's Highway 1, climbed Mount St. Helens in Washington, and celebrated her fiftieth birthday by skydiving. She snow-skied, water-skied, hiked, and completed a short-course triathlon. But Maggie racked up no adventures this February, the month when she first wore the necklace. Unlike the others, she couldn't celebrate her first turn with the diamonds. She had to focus all her energies on making a living and remaking a life.

Maggie had plenty of experience remaking a life. Her marriage to her college boyfriend had ended after five years when he wanted children and she wanted a career. With her second husband, she filed after three months and two shoves.

Those dissolutions paled beside the one she was going through when it was her turn to wear the diamonds. This divorce was dissolving sixteen years of marriage to the father of her two children. The split had thrown her into a depression, and the joint custody agreement continued to wring her dry. She'd kissed her kids good night every night since they were born. Now she'd see them only every other week. She knew she'd have to find new activities. She didn't like being alone at the end of a workday.

But her support network had shrunk. With the marital split, she'd lost couple friends. Worse, she'd lost her husband's family, who for sixteen years had been her family, too.

Her own parents were dead. One brother languished in a prison mental ward. Her three other siblings lived in the Midwest. Growing up in Chicago, Maggie had enjoyed a close group of girlfriends, from grammar school through high school, but those friends had all stayed in Chicago.

Friends from former jobs—and former lives—were scattered from New York to Arizona. Even her workplaces were shrinking. She was selling homes for a real estate company with only five people in the office. As she got older, she'd discovered, life became harder to start anew.

She'd met Jonell at a seminar and had known instantly she wanted to buy a share of the necklace. Now here she was at the end of February, "her month," hosting the group to cede the diamonds that hadn't been anywhere. Letting go of the necklace wouldn't be hard. Why, she could barely remember wearing it. With the separation and move to the rental house, the month had bogged into chaos. Moving was always an ordeal, but not having her children for the first time was torture. An added misery: The necklace was hers for Valentine's Day, but she'd had no one to go out with on the most romantic night of the year. Getting through the holidays, she'd seen then, was going to be tough. She'd loved hosting seasonal parties for her husband's family.

That was gone now. All that remained was a profound sense of disconnection.

At six the night of the meeting, the women sauntered in talking and laughing. They hugged Maggie. "Your house looks great," said one after another. Their compliments made the necklace exchange seem more like a housewarming. Maggie had spent only a few hours with these women, and yet, as she looked around her living room, she felt befriended in a way she hadn't in a long time. There was some good in this month after all. The necklace had brought a new energy into her life. Maybe the necklace would lead her to a new chapter, she thought.

She hoped.

AS THE MONTHS PASSED, Maggie struggled to deepen the connection she felt that night at her house. But friendship didn't come as quickly or as easily as Maggie had anticipated. In so many ways, she was different from the other women. For one thing, she looked different. While most of them showed some sign of a softer shape, Maggie, the youngest of the group, displayed the hard body of a thirty-year-old. While most of the others had chosen to age naturally, Maggie had opted for eyelid surgery and a face-lift.

There were differences that weren't superficial. Most of the women could count long-term friends among them, while Maggie knew only three women—casually. Maggie was the only mom in the group still raising children, ten and fifteen, which meant she sometimes came late to meetings because she had to attend parent-teacher conferences and baseball and softball games. Then, too, she missed a lot of the conversation because she was hearing-impaired. She was grateful for her hearing aids, which she'd worn since she was thirty, but the hearing loss she loathed. She missed out on jokes. Whispers were impossible. When the women all talked at once, and they often all talked at once, Maggie couldn't hear.

But she could hardly wait for her second go-round with the necklace. This time she'd do it right. She vowed to make it an adventure as only Maggie, the adventuress, could. She planned to skydive again. The first time had been such a rush that she'd adhered a bumper sticker on her Town and Country van that read: "Skydive! Take risks, not to escape life but to prevent life from escaping."

Maggie set a date, then e-mailed KCBS-TV, Channel 2 in Los Angeles. "I'll be skydiving wearing Jewelia, a $37,000 diamond necklace. I think it's a great story. Let me know if you're interested."

A producer at the station e-mailed back, "We're interested."

On a breezy, sunny day in February, Maggie drove 140 miles to the Jim Wallace Skydiving School in Perris, California. She exchanged small talk for a few minutes with the reporter and cameraman. Then she wiggled into a jumpsuit of periwinkle blue polycotton. She strapped on a harness. She put on gloves and goggles. Then she secured the diamond necklace to the back of her neck with duct tape.

"I'm going to have one of those 'airgasms' today," she vamped to the camera with a smile that broadened into a rich laugh as she added, "Jewelia's about to jump out of an airplane for the very first time."

The camera zoomed in on Maggie's fine features, her green eyes, her blond, wispy hair, the diamonds ringing her neck. As the wind blew, the camera caught the $10.99 rhinestone studs she'd bought at JCPenney to go with the necklace.

Maggie gave a thumbs-up, then boarded the DHC-6 aircraft. She found a place on the bench seat between two other jumpers.

The plane took off. One by one, the skydivers did too.

"Your turn," the instructor said to Maggie.

She rose from her seat. The instructor harnessed his body to hers.

"I'm ready," she said, smiling again for the camera.

She leaned out the side of the plane. At thirteen thousand feet, she jumped.

Maggie's body went horizontal, her legs and arms flailing wide. She blew a kiss for the camera. She plummeted at 120 miles per hour, free-falling for fifty seconds, the wind roaring in her ears.

Then she pulled the ripcord. The parachute opened. Her body went vertical. The next five thousand feet were soundless and serene as Maggie and Jewelia floated to the ground.

Maggie arose from the soft landing, untangling herself from the harness and the instructor. "That was awesome," she effused to the camera.

She groped for the necklace. "Jewelia made it. She survived her first skydive."

When the tape stopped rolling, Maggie asked the reporter when the segment would air. Probably within a few days, he said, on the five P.M. news.

Each afternoon, Maggie set her TiVo to record the news, and on the third day after her jump, the segment aired. Seeing the TV clip, she experienced the high all over again. She replayed the recording three times. She couldn't wait to show it to the group. Finally, she'd had an adventure with the necklace, something to connect her to the others. And she'd showcased Jewelia to a TV audience of millions. The women would be thrilled.

TWO NIGHTS LATER, Maggie greeted the women with hugs and high spirits. She sat patiently through dinner and the agenda.

Finally, Jonell turned to Maggie. "Well, how was your month with Jewelia?"

"Awesome," said Maggie. "I'll show you." She turned on her thirty-five-inch Sony TV to play the segment. She stood back to watch. Yes, again: This was one video she wouldn't tire of watching. She loved seeing herself perform death-defying acts.

As the women watched, the temperature in the room took a dive, too. Most hadn't seen the segment on TV. Most hadn't known about the skydive.

Many were thinking the same thing: *What's she doing? Where'd she get the idea that this experiment was about her being on television?*

The clip ended. No one spoke.

The silence told Maggie that she'd dropped a bomb, but she had no idea how. When Patti took Jewelia boogie-boarding in Hawaii, everyone wanted to hear about it. When Dale took the diamonds to Paris, everyone was interested. Why wasn't anyone interested in Maggie's adventure?

Baffled and hurt, Maggie didn't say anything, either.

Minutes after the clip dissolved, so did the meeting.

Over the next few days, through calls and e-mails, the women decided that Jonell would e-mail Maggie to communicate the message from the group: You can wear the necklace to do whatever you want, to skydive or bungee jump or rappel from a mountain, but don't alert the media. Personal promotion is not what we're about.

Reading the e-mail, Maggie's muscles tensed, which made the veins in her arms bulge. Now Maggie was the one taken aback. She was quick to call Jonell and just as quick to pounce in her defense. After all, she'd acted no differently from the way she always had. She'd called the newspapers when unsafe surfing practices almost killed her daughter. She sent out mass mailings to promote activities of her ski club. She'd contacted every Ventura media outlet for the "Million Mom March" in L.A. Media was her background. She'd majored in communications in college in Minnesota. She'd reported for the CBS affiliate in La Crosse, Wisconsin. She'd written audiovisual scripts and sold radio ads. Until she'd started selling homes, her entire working life had been in media.

Jonell remembered Maggie's background from early introductions, but she listened again. "You can tell the women how you feel at the next meeting," she said kindly. "We can talk more about it then."

Maggie didn't feel like sitting on the hot seat to hear twelve women tell her she'd screwed up. She didn't go to the meeting but stayed home, where she spent the evening thinking about this turn of events.

Maggie could not be on the outs with these women. She was on the outs with her ex, her ex's family, and now her teenage daughter. Maggie'd had such high hopes for the group. She would not—could not—lose her connection with them. She e-mailed the most sincere apology she could write. But within the two pages, she volleyed criticism right back at the women: In the future, she wrote, if you have a complaint about me, tell me directly—not behind my back.

As she clicked the "send" icon, Maggie realized she'd been a solo operator for so long that she'd forgotten what being part of a group meant. She hadn't had to clear her activities with anyone since she'd been—what?—eleven.

That year, Maggie's alcoholic father died, leaving their family with a year's worth of overdue rent and thousands of dollars in medical bills, but zero dollars in the bank. Within the year, her mother succumbed to the illness of alcoholism, too, officially ending Maggie's childhood.

The oldest of five, she had to be home every day after school, making sure her younger brothers and sisters did their homework and chores. At fourteen, she'd needed money for clothes and contact lenses, so she started working twenty-four hours a week selling candy at the Chicago Theatre, the biggest movie house downtown. That she had to walk through a rough neighborhood at eleven P.M. on weeknights and at two A.M. on weekends didn't deter her. She learned to swear in Spanish. She practiced tough looks in the mirror until she'd mastered a sneer that said, "Don't mess with me." She stood five feet, four inches, and weighed one hundred pounds, but no one ever bothered her.

She'd worked ever since those nights in downtown Chicago. She'd worked her way through college with student loans and waitressing jobs. She'd never looked to anyone for support or advice or as a sounding board.

None of the women mentioned the incident again. Neither did Maggie. But she thought long and hard about what had happened.

First she looked inward. She knew her bluntness, set in motion on the mean streets of Chicago, could offend. So could the arrogance she'd developed from being a TV reporter for three years, interviewing such famous folk as Jimmy Carter and Nancy Reagan. She was going to have to act differently with these women, she concluded, think before she spoke, think before she acted. She'd have to soften her edges.

Maggie wasn't easily discouraged. She just faced a new challenge, that's all. And when hadn't Maggie risen to a challenge? When the real estate market slumped, she complained like every other real estate agent in the country, then she took action. She invested twenty-five hundred dollars in a real estate coach, made plans to get her broker's license, and moved to a more upbeat office environment. She decided to become certified as a personal trainer, and she started teaching a twelve-week workshop, "Living a Life of Fitness and Health (No Matter What)."

MAVERICKS IS A GYM on Telegraph Road, across from the mall, where Maggie's a regular. She's just finished a thirty-minute weight-lifting session. She's wearing faded black stretch workout pants, a fitted tank top that bares her whittled midriff, and Nike Air cross-trainers. She's added fifteen pounds of muscle since her teen years, but she's still thin, still petite. A fine sheen of sweat covers her skin.

"Wearing the necklace when I'm going out all dressed up—that feels glamorous," she says. "Wearing it to the gym when I'm in sweaty workout clothes and no makeup, that's fun.

"I started working out twenty-six years ago when I was running a department and was so stressed I couldn't sleep at night. At the gym I discovered it was just me and the equipment. I didn't hear phones ringing, didn't see piles of work. It became a form of meditation. When I saw how working out de-stressed me, I made a commitment. I kept workout clothes in the car and went straight from work to the gym twice a week. People look at me and think I must work out every day. I don't, but I do work out consistently and have for half my life. Commitment is the number one word in my vocabulary.

"The other reason I work out is that I need the energy because I have young kids. I've got a ten-year-old I shoot hoops with. If I don't stay fit I won't be able to do what I want to do when I'm older. When I travel I won't be able to climb steps to a palace I want to see. If I need surgery and I'm not fit, it'll take longer to recover.

"Everyone in my family died by the age of seventy-five. That's too short a life for me. I've got to stay fit to beat those odds because I'll be sixty when my son's in college. I might be seventy before I'm a grandmother. And I've gotta take those grandkids to Disneyland.

"New adventures—that's the other key to staying young. I take every opportunity to try something new. That's also what Jewelia was about for me. My next adventure is climbing Mount Whitney, the highest peak in the lower forty-eight states. I'm committed. I'll get to the top if I have to crawl.

"I work just as hard on my mind as I work on my body. I've been reading books on personal transformation since the eighties when I read *Success Through a Positive Mental Attitude* by Napoleon Hill and W. Clement Stone. I have affirmations on Post-its all over my bathroom mirror and my bedpost. I'm constantly working on myself to get rid of the past, to live a healthy, authentic life. Some days it's easy. Other days, not so easy.

"Sometimes in this group I feel insignificant and unheard. I have to combat that feeling. I have to tell myself, 'These are wonderful women. Feeling insignificant and unheard is your past.'

"You have to clear out the past, clear out all negativity. If I hadn't done so much work on myself, I wouldn't have been able to handle the fallout from the skydiving incident. This group is like any relationship. And the foundation of a great relationship is a commitment to work through the problems.

"In the beginning of a conflict, our finger points out in blame, but ultimately we have to point it at ourselves and take responsibility. I realized if I want deep friendships among these women, I have to reach out. You can't get to know someone once a month. Meeting people one on one is the way to build relationships. I intend to call every woman to have lunch. I live by my goals, and one of them is to feel a part of this group. I'm committed.

"Women friends are essential to a healthy life."

CHAPTER SIX

Tina Osborne, the reluctant

...

Finding joy in making a difference

O N JANUARY 2, 2005, THE *VENTURA COUNTY STAR*
published a news feature on the thirteen women and their
diamond necklace. Two days later, the paper ran a letter to
the editor written by a former Harvard professor, who was
teaching at California Lutheran University. He lambasted the
women. "A good example of how the media promote the false
idea that the ownership of stuff and self-aggrandizement will
bring happiness," he wrote. "Wearing the necklace in public
involves another problem: the display of feigned wealth."

Reading the letter, Jonell felt chagrined. Were the professor's words true? Were the women pretending to be
more than they were? On her cell phone, on her morning
walks, with friends and family, Jonell talked and expanded
and expounded. Mortification quickly gave way to amusement, that a psychology professor would take the time to
comment on her experiment. And then amusement gave
way to argument. Jonell loved to spar.

"Well, of course, the media promote the false idea that
ownership of stuff brings happiness. This is news? But
that's not what we're about. And what's the problem with
the display of feigned wealth? And who defines wealth anyway? Maybe the sharing is the real wealth. How about that?"

The more she talked, the more questions she asked. Finally, one remained: "Can we make this necklace mean something more?"

The professor's words may have rankled, but they also spurred her to action.

TWO MONTHS LATER, on March 8, 2005, International Women's Day, the group threw a party. The goal: to raise money for Ventura's Coalition to End Family Violence. The lure: An Evening with Jewelia.

The women decided to keep it simple, to print flyers on $8\frac{1}{2}$-×-11-inch computer paper, to distribute them to families, friends, co-workers, and businesses. To charm friends and acquaintances into donating the space, the staff, the music, the wine, the flowers, the food: platters of bruschetta and exotic cheeses, quiches of goat cheese and sun-dried tomatoes, miniature tarts of figs and cherries. The women coaxed two husbands into tending bar and gave two homeless men twenty dollars to carry in the beer.

Many of the women had been involved in fund-raisers before, but those had been major planned events. For this one they were flying by the seat of their capris. As with anything put together in a few weeks, the little bash raised the anxiety level before it raised funds: What if we give a party and no one comes? With neither R.S.V.P. enclosure cards nor follow-up calls, the women could only wonder: Will ten people show up, or might two hundred, with not enough bruschetta to go around?

Norbert Furnee, gourmet, oenophile, and bon vivant, had offered Deco, his chic continental restaurant downtown. Just around the corner from where Erle Stanley Gardner penned his Perry Mason novels, Deco was ensconced on the first floor of the historic Bank of Italy building, its bas-relief exterior crafted of Italian marble.

Deco wasn't the first restaurant in Ventura with fine dining, but Furnee's place was perhaps the first restaurant with such flair: walls painted sage green, a ceiling the color of butternut squash, a bar hand-built of Philippine mahogany, contemporary art from the owner's private collection, a formidable wine menu.

At five o'clock, people started arriving. By five-thirty, guests were so jammed against one another in the tiny space that they overflowed past the enclosed patio onto the sidewalk. With the noise level rising and elbows jostling, the women started to relax. They squeezed through the crowd, greeting new arrivals. "Where's Jewelia?" asked one guest after another. The women scanned the room, then mouthed the words to one another: Where *is* Jewelia?

The women knew that Tina Osborne had the diamonds this month. What the women didn't know was that Tina didn't want to go to the fund-raiser. Tina wanted to drop out of the group altogether.

TWO HOURS EARLIER, while the women of Jewelia were reconfiguring Deco's tables for maximum mingling, Tina Osborne was ending her day at Our Lady of the Assumption, a parochial middle school on Telegraph Road, across from the mall. There, Tina taught social studies, spelling, and religion.

Student art, a UCLA banner, a poster of Jesus, and a crucifix decorated the walls of her large, sunny classroom. But there was little sign that some ninety students had used the room that day—not a stray paper or book in sight, each chair placed precisely on top of a desk.

At five feet, one inch, Tina didn't stand much taller than her students, but her small stature housed a big voice and a commanding presence. With her blond hair, deep tan, flat sandals, and short, floral skirt, she epitomized the "California casual" look. Her attitude, however, was all business. She didn't let her students leave until the classroom was as orderly as when they had arrived. When she chastised them—"I am not happy with you"—they paid attention. No matter how stern her expression, it couldn't hide her beauty. Her features were so exquisite, so perfectly proportioned, they could have been on a movie screen.

Tina's day had been a long one. She'd rehearsed her seventh graders for a Lenten Passion Mass. She'd enlivened the study of ancient Egypt for her sixth graders by working with them to mummify a chicken, then bury it in the schoolyard. She prepared her eighth graders for a mock trial and explained to them manifest destiny in nineteenth-century America. She tested her seventh graders on spelling, and although Tina was beat, she was staying after school to grade the spelling tests. Sometimes she stayed as late as five-thirty. Her policy? Never take work home. She wanted a life beyond the classroom.

Lately, however, that life seemed to be narrowing.

Three doors from her own, her ninety-two-year-old mother was failing, her eyes increasingly vacant. Having a live-in caretaker was a blessing, but Tina still bought her mom's groceries and medicines, took her dinner during the week, and visited almost every afternoon after school. The only girl among seven brothers, Tina had bonded with her mother at an early age. Her mother had been the one woman Tina could always confide in. Those days were gone.

And now, when Tina went home after school, the man waiting for her was no longer the man she'd fallen in love with at UCLA, the dental student who'd served her meals at the Theta house, the man who'd reminded her of her brothers: handsome, cocky, fun, quick. Ozzie was still handsome, but he was no longer quick. Ozzie had Parkinson's. He was fifty-eight.

"WHEN I HEARD the diagnosis, I was shocked. It's one thing to have a parent be ill, but someone your own age hits you differently. At first I felt bad for him. Then, I thought, what happens if he doesn't work? I knew he'd have to retire his dental practice. He'd get two years of disability, but what about after that? Would we be able to make it financially?

"I had to go back to teaching full-time. I don't know when I'll be able to retire. We need the medical benefits. Neither of us comes from affluent families. Finances are always a worry.

"I started teaching when my youngest child was in seventh grade. I liked working because it gave me my own money. I did whatever I wanted with it, which usually meant buying things for the house, which was great. Now it goes into the pot, which has been hard. I can't hide it in my bra drawer anymore.

"Overnight our roles reversed. All of a sudden I had to

be the provider. I resented that. I felt I should be living another kind of life.

"I didn't tell anyone about his diagnosis for a long time—no one at school, none of my friends or family. I just wanted to pull in. It was too new, too private. I didn't want people talking about us.

"I was afraid. Of losing him. Of surviving financially. I'd wake up at two A.M. with my mind racing. Will we be able to stay in our house? What if we can't? Where will we go? I'd reach for my rosary and pray. Please God, show me the way. I wouldn't fall back asleep until five A.M. Half an hour later, I had to drag myself out of bed to go to work.

"Then I became angry. Why us? Why me? I already had my mom to take care of. I was angry because I was doing more and more, and I was maxed out.

"It's hard to see his deterioration. He gets a serious look on his face, a mask, and I think he's mad at me or uninterested in what I'm saying. That look is neither. It's just part of the disease. You get angry at the person who's ill because their personality changes. You lose the person you married. You lose your best friend.

"More and more, I feel a separation. Between who he was and who he is. Between who he is and who I am. We're no longer going in the same direction.

"All of a sudden my mother's really old and my husband's getting old, and psychologically you can become old when you're around old people. *But I'm not there yet.* And I don't want to get there. I'm a young personality. I look young. I don't have any physical problems. I don't take any medications.

"I go to my mom's after school but she's not communicating, then I come home and my husband's not communicating as he used to, and I feel so lonely. I'm sandwiched between two overwhelming sadnesses. I have a knot in my stomach all the time.

"Having to socialize with this new group of women felt like one more thing."

TINA HADN'T PARTICIPATED in any of the preparations for the fund-raising event. She hadn't sent out invitations to family or friends or co-workers. She told Ozzie that the fund-raiser didn't seem that important. He could go or not. He opted out.

Tina wanted to opt out, too. She didn't want to be with anyone, much less a crowd. She'd been reluctant to join the group in the first place. Groups had never interested Tina, and she already had friends. Plus, she didn't know most of these women. Having to get to know them felt like more work. The only reason she'd joined was that Nancy Huff had talked her into it.

Tonight's event puzzled Tina. No one had talked to her about it. No one had asked if she was going. So how important could it be?

As she mulled over that question, her Catholic guilt kicked in. The event was happening during her month with the necklace. She might as well wear it out. She certainly hadn't worn it to school. Well, technically she had, but she'd hidden the diamonds under turtlenecks and collared shirts. She felt self-conscious wearing it in front of the other teachers.

Tina tried on a few outfits, settling on a straight black lace skirt and a clinging black jersey wrap with a V neckline plunging into a very unteacherly décolletage. She slipped on black sequined high-heeled sandals. She freshened her makeup by adding a darker eye shadow and redder lipstick. She fluffed her short, frosted hair, then tucked it behind her ears. She added diamond studs that had been her mother's. The diamond necklace already circled her neck, but with this outfit the jewels made sense. With this outfit, they dazzled. Tina checked herself in the full-length mirror and liked what she saw: The no-nonsense teacher morphed into a glamour girl. Tina didn't like to party or drink during the week, but after she'd worked all day, dressing up felt good.

At five-thirty, Tina reached Deco. She found a parking place in front of the building, as though the traffic gods were smiling on her. She climbed out of her white Volvo station wagon and walked toward the pavement. Flashbulbs popped. Unfamiliar faces smiled. Voices shouted, "She's arrived! . . . Give her room . . . Here she comes . . . Isn't she lovely?"

Tina looked around her. Who was everyone talking about? Were they talking about her? Why would everyone be waiting for her? What was going on?

The voices grew louder: "gorgeous . . . exquisite . . . spectacular."

My gosh, thought Tina, *don't tell me they're talking about my breasts.* She knew her neckline showed cleavage, but she didn't think it was excessive. But why else would so many men be staring at her chest?

"Come over here . . . over here . . . can I take a picture with you? . . . I want a picture with Jewelia."

Jewelia! Of course. People weren't talking about her. They were talking about the diamond necklace. Okay girl, she thought, rally to the cause. Pull your shoulders back, your boobs up. Flash that smile.

Tina flashed a dazzling one. She knew how to walk the red carpet.

SHE'D WALKED IT when she was crowned homecoming queen at Mary Star of the Sea, her Catholic high school in San Pedro. She'd walked it in front of coaches and athletes when they named her runner-up for Miss UCLA. And she'd walked it when a committee of four men chose her for her dream summer gig in college: cocktail waitress at Walt Disney's Club 33, an exclusive dining club for visiting dignitaries. The job required a French maid costume but generated the biggest tips at Disneyland.

The job wasn't an odd fantasy for a girl growing up in Los Angeles, twenty miles from Hollywood. A touch of glamour permeated Tina's home life. In her eyes, her strikingly attractive parents resembled movie stars. Tina's standard line had always been "My mom looks like Elizabeth Taylor and my dad like John Wayne." Two of Tina's seven brothers had acted in a movie as kids, one in a TV series. Tina used to spend three afternoons a week and all day Saturday practicing ballet at the dance studio of famous fifties dancer Cyd Charisse's husband, Nico. Tina had loved recitals. She'd loved being onstage. After she'd seen *Captain January*, she'd asked her dad to please call her Star, after Shirley Temple's character. And that's what her dad called her until the day he died.

Tina's family was still in the limelight. One brother worked as a cinematographer; one taught acting and sang professionally; one performed with a band. And now the klieg lights had lured the next generation. Tina's son Sean produced extreme-sports TV shows for the networks. Her daughter Mary had won the MTV reality show *Surf Girls*, which led to appearances in commercials, magazine features, and documentaries.

Tina was content to let her children be the stars now. She'd stopped thinking about center stage long ago.

THE FUND-RAISER WAS supposed to end at eight P.M., but at eight people stood five deep at the bar, circles of guests moving like a sweep hand on a watch, everyone in flux. Tina thought she knew almost everyone in Ventura, but the room was filled with new faces. All evening, people approached her, talked to her, wanted to hear the story of the necklace. Tina didn't tire of telling the story. All evening, people wanted to take her picture. Tina didn't tire of smiling.

At nine-thirty people were still mingling and pressing the flesh, and Tina was still "on." She hated for the night to end, but at ten, she finally drove home. On the way, she said a prayer of gratitude that she'd worn the right outfit—even more, that she'd shown up.

She couldn't wait to talk about the evening. But Ozzie was already asleep. And ten-thirty P.M. was too late to call anyone without feeling guilty about waking them, so she e-mailed a friend. Tina replayed the entire evening—the crowd, the spontaneity, the energy. Feeling like a movie star. Feeling like a blithe spirit.

"It was magical," she tapped out, this time with her hands doing the dancing. "A night I'll never forget."

A night that kept Tina in the group.

"BY OUR FIFTIES," Tina reflected later, "if we're engaged with life, something's happened. Never did I imagine that I'd be as busy today working and caregiving as I was when raising four children. So many women as they get older hold on to their anger and become bitter, the lines on their faces drawing them down. I was determined not to become like that. When I start to feel myself thinking negative thoughts I know it's time to go out with the girls."

CHAPTER SEVEN

Mary Osborn, the competitor

. . .

Aiming for empowerment

A . . .

AT THE SAME TIME THAT TINA WAS ENJOYING HER moment in the spotlight, another glamorous blonde was squeezing her way through the crowd. She shared Tina's last name but little else. Where Tina was petite, Mary Osborn was statuesque. Where Tina was still with her first husband, Mary was on her third marriage. Where Tina had spent her working life in education, Mary had spent hers in business. But the happening at Deco aroused in the two women the same reaction: a reassessment of the group's value.

Mary had been one of the many who'd flatly turned down Jonell's proposition. The idea that women could share a diamond necklace seemed preposterous to her. Everyone would want to wear it at the same time. Mary could envision catfights, but she couldn't envision a single activity in her life where she'd wear such a thing.

Now here she was, a guest at the fund-raiser, startled that the women were not just using the necklace to raise money for a worthy cause, but they were also socializing with friends and family and meeting interesting, new people. All in just a few hours.

Boy, that's maximizing discretionary time, thought Mary

enviously. She'd obviously made a mistake by not signing on, but she didn't have to live with it. She could change the situation.

Later, at a meeting of her investment club, of which several Jewelia women were members, she sought out Jonell first.

"I want in," she said. "First woman who leaves, I want in."

Mary then made her way toward the others in the necklace coterie. "If anyone ever wants out," she said, "please use your influence to get me in."

One month later, a woman left the group and Mary joined it.

MARY OSBORN KNEW how to work a crowd. At a motorcycle-rights political function, she maneuvered her way through some 150 bikers to meet the speaker who'd impressed her. After discovering they shared a love of Harleys and politics, she married him. As a member of the Central Committee of the Ventura County Republican Party, she regularly performed the "meet and greet" routine with visiting politicians. As senior executive assistant to the CEO of Behavioral Science Technology, Inc., an international safety consulting company headquartered in Ojai, she met VIPs and staffers from across the country.

Mary excelled in meeting new people. With her evenly modulated voice, her measured words, her composed demeanor, she exuded the kind of poise that defines Miss Americas. With her delicately pretty features and Vegas showgirl body, she could also have held her own in the swimsuit competition. In the office, wearing power suits, silks, and heels, she personified professionalism.

Not wanting to hold her back, her boss encouraged her to apply for a public relations position in the company. But Mary enjoyed what she termed her "Girl Friday job," where she did everything for her boss from juggling his calendar to preparing his presentations. She enjoyed being close to the power, on the inside where decisions were made; she'd found gratification working for a man she continued to learn from. Plus, she was compensated for the ten- to twelve-hour days with a salary that placed her in the top 4 percent of women wage earners.

Mary didn't like to wear the diamonds at the office. The necklace didn't feel like an appropriate accoutrement for a corporate culture. She did, however, enjoy wearing it on the open road while astraddle her Harley-Davidson Low Rider. She also enjoyed wearing it at the gun range.

AFTER A FIFTY-HOUR workweek Mary is spending her Saturday at a "Women on Target" workshop at the Ojai Valley Gun Club. She's been a member of the club for six years and a member of the National Rifle Association for twelve.

The gun range is located in Los Padres National Forest on the outskirts of Ojai, a city twenty minutes from Ventura. The mountains around Ojai were used as the site of Shangri-La in Frank Capra's 1937 film of James Hilton's novel *Lost Horizon*. The gun range chokes in dusty desert. No "misty mountains" within miles. Here, amid sagebrush and scrub, the grass straggles, the heat oppresses.

Despite this parched setting, Mary is the embodiment of

"cool." She's wearing snug blue jeans, a black long-sleeved shirt, a black baseball cap with a gold NRA logo, Juicy Couture sunglasses—and a 118-diamond necklace. Her black boots with two-inch heels shoot her up to six feet tall. Mary looks a decade younger than her fifty-nine years—way too young for a sixteen-year-old boy to be calling her Grandma. She recalls such pistol-packing babes as Julie Christie in *McCabe & Mrs. Miller* and Jane Fonda in *Cat Ballou.*

Mary makes her way to her men friends, most of whom are working today as instructors. She knows them from trapshooting at the club on weekends with her husband, and she hugs one after another. She circulates among the women, too, encouraging them to become club members. "I firmly believe we have the right to protect ourselves," she tells a woman shooting for the first time. "When my husband leaves town I feel more confident having a gun."

The NRA-sponsored "women only" workshop is a first for the club. The clinic is full, with twenty-seven women ranging in age from teenagers to sixty-year-olds. Participants and instructors help themselves to coffee and blueberry muffins, then congregate at wooden picnic tables in the covered shelter.

Mary navigates this rough-hewn environment as easily and smoothly as she does her refined workplace. Not surprising, since she grew up on military bases, where her father was a career serviceman who started in the navy and segued to the air force. He presented Mary and her two older sisters each with a Red Ryder BB gun, then took his girls out to the fields to teach them to shoot. Mary's mother, a good shot herself, sometimes joined them. Mary's father was away so much that these times with him were memorable, all the more so because they were short-lived. He died when Mary was nine.

That BB gun is long gone, but her interest in firearms stayed. Today Mary owns a 12-gauge shotgun, "a beautiful Beretta"; a High Standard Supermatic Trophy .22; a Colt Combat Commander; a Desert Eagle handgun; and, for sentimental reasons, two Red Ryders. She signed up for the workshop because she'd never taken a class in pistol shooting.

The seminar starts, with one instructor assigned to two students. Mary is paired with Stephanie Fuller, a fifty-two-year-old mortgage loan processor. The two women sit across the table from their instructor, Ralph Rendina, an auto mechanic and competitive shooter. He's tanned and muscular, with short spiked hair.

"There is no safety in a firearm," he says. "You are the safety. Thirty years ago people learned about firearms from their families. Today they learn about them from Hollywood, and in the movies firearms are handled all wrong."

As Rendina lectures, Mary takes off her sunglasses and tucks them into the V of her shirt. She shows Rendina the gun she's brought, her husband's Colt Python .357 Magnum. "We share our handguns," she says.

Rendina demonstrates the proper grip, trigger squeeze, the technique to load and unload. Mary sits rapt. When he drops a bullet, she jumps up to retrieve it.

Though instructing two women, Rendina focuses his eyes and questions on Mary.

"If you were afraid for your life," he asks her, "would you shoot someone?"

"Oh yeah," she says in a nanosecond.

"Then you need to learn defensive shooting."

"That would be fun," she says. "Are there classes for women?"

ON THE SHOOTING RANGE, twenty targets are lined up at fifty feet. Mary puts on protective glasses and earmuffs. She and Stephanie alternate taking aim. Rendina talks and teaches all the while.

"The best sharpshooters are women," he says. "Their heart and respiratory rates are slower than men's, so they're steadier."

Mary fires off a total of twenty-three rounds. She shoots one-handed, two-handed, right-handed, and left-handed. She varies the angle of her stance. Though none of her shots hits the black center, every one of them lands within the score rings.

After the shooting ends for the morning, Rendina walks up to each of the twenty targets to peer closely at the markings. "As for consistency," he concludes, "Mary's target is the best one out here."

"Shooting invigorates me," she says afterward, elegantly sipping from a can of diet Pepsi. "I'd love to shoot every weekend. It's a wonderful sport. I could never get the women of Jewelia to do this, but wouldn't it be fun to go out with your girlfriends and shoot guns?"

"I'M VERY COMPETITIVE," Mary says a few days after the gun clinic. "Each time I shoot I want to do better. I wanted to do better than Stephanie.

"I was gangly and awkward growing up so I didn't play sports. My second husband was a competitive power-lifter. He got me into target shooting, bodybuilding, arm wrestling. We had an arm wrestling table at home, and I entered competitions. He's the one who got me interested in motorcycles.

"I like being in control of powerful machines. I like cars with powerful motors. I drove a race car once at Lyons Drag Strip in L.A., did a quarter mile in ten seconds. I like the adrenaline rush that comes from taking risks. And I like the sense of empowerment.

"My competitiveness is probably an outgrowth of the fact that I didn't have an opportunity to go to college, or if I did, I didn't see it. After my father died, my mother suffered emotional struggles. I went to four different high schools. I was desperate to get out of my home life so I left home at seventeen, got married at eighteen, had my first daughter at twenty-two. With the exception of one year after she was born, I've worked full-time since I was eighteen.

"I so wanted my daughters to go to college. I didn't want them to make my mistakes. But they both did exactly what I did, and it broke my heart. I've learned that it's more important what you model to your children than what you say to them.

"I've been haunted by not having a degree. It's why I've worked hard to get an informal education. I'm always seeking new information, always taking a class in something— Great Books seminars, legislative workshops, computer classes. One of my husband's attractions is that he challenges me intellectually. I can't get enough learning. I'm always asking myself, 'What do college grads know that I don't?'

"Some days I think a degree isn't that important anymore. I've met lots of people with degrees who aren't as smart as I am. Other days, I think that I cannot die without a degree. I know that getting one would improve my self-esteem. People often ask where I went to school or what my degree is in. I'm always embarrassed. They marginalize me, even today. The result is that when I first met these women, I felt intimidated.

"So many of them were sorority girls and debutantes and graduate students while I was coping with two difficult husbands and raising babies. I've never had the women to my home, so humble compared to their houses.

"Generally we choose friends of like minds. If I hadn't joined this group I never would have met half these women. Jonell's liberalism was hard for me. I've always thought 1968 was the major dividing line for our generation. I thought it was disgraceful that people were protesting the Vietnam War, and with such anger. How could they be so disrespectful to soldiers and government? During the course of working with a life coach, I asked his help in understanding her. He gave me an article on the sixties' counterculture, which opened my eyes.

"I'm a black-and-white person. I don't see too much gray. Listening to the women's different viewpoints has made me less narrow-minded. They've broadened my outlook. They've given me a course in Group Dynamics 101. And they're so empowered themselves that being with them has been empowering for me."

—

ONE YEAR AFTER joining the women of Jewelia, Mary per-
suaded the group to adopt Miracle House as its next fund-
raiser. Miracle House provided an intensive, residential
drug-rehab program for women. Ever since the program
had saved the life of someone in Mary's family, she'd
wanted to give back. One of these days, someday, maybe,
she'd tell herself. But she had no idea what to do.

With this group of women, she knew just what to do. She
took charge of the fund-raiser, just as she'd taken charge of
company events over the years.

This function was markedly different from the one at
Deco. Rain pelted the rooftop of Table 13, a much bigger
restaurant, which gave the feel of a much smaller crowd.
But that didn't matter. What the evening lacked in atmosphere, it made up for in poignancy, as two women gave
tearful testimonials. Their stories, crediting Miracle House
with saving their lives, moved the crowd, including a tearful Mary. With the women of Jewelia she'd realized a dream.

The fifty-dollar donations at the door netted seventy-
five hundred dollars for the organization. At Deco, the donations to the Coalition to End Family Violence totaled
fifty-four hundred dollars. Neither take was a huge sum of
money, but it was money that would make a difference.

The coalition used the money to provide ninety days of
play therapy for children at its shelter who'd been victims of
domestic abuse. Miracle House was able to subsidize ten
women who needed treatment but couldn't afford it. "We'd

just had a funding cut," said director Brenda Davison, "so the money they raised felt like it came from heaven."

Astonished by the ease with which thirteen women working together could make an impact, the group found a direction: grassroots philanthropy in the community, where the women knew the needs and could see the results.

A year and a half after they'd joined together, the women of Jewelia had raised more money with their diamond necklace than they had spent buying it.

CHAPTER EIGHT

Mary Karrh, the pragmatist

...

Rediscovering a passionate life

J ONELL HANDED OUT A MEETING AGENDA WITH HER USUAL
mischief:

1. Where has Jewelia been—in lots of interesting
   places—in cold water and between oh how many legs?
2. Where is she going next?
3. Who can she help?
4. Is everybody happy?

In one way, yes, everyone was happy. The fund-raisers
gratified the women. An article about Jewelia in *People*
magazine thrilled them. But some women felt that outside
forces were coming into play and that, clearly, the group
needed protection in the form of a limited liability company, an LLC.

Jonell was astonished.

"Why would we need such a thing?" she asked.

"What if someone comes to one of our fund-raisers and
sues us?" someone answered.

"I've been sued as a real estate agent and I've been sued
as a neighbor," Jonell countered. "But I still wouldn't sue
anyone. I hate that the world works that way."

"But that's the way the world works," someone responded.

"I know that's the way the world works," Jonell said. "My real estate contracts contain eighteen pages of disclosures. But this isn't business as usual. We're a group of women sharing a *necklace.*"

But the businesswomen among them wanted business as usual. They wanted rules of operation.

Jonell didn't like rules. From the get-go, she'd chanted, "The only rule will be no rules."

Someone said, "No rules is a rule."

"That's true," Jonell ceded. "But let's have one place in our lives without more rules."

"What if a woman wants out?" someone asked. "Can she decide who to give her share to, or does the group decide? And what part of her original investment does she get back?"

"We'll figure it out when the time comes."

Jonell wanted to wing it. Others wanted to lay down principles to avoid jumping from crisis to crisis. To them, written agreements smoothed human interactions.

Jonell quoted Katharine Hepburn: "Follow all the rules, miss all the fun." Rules limit the possibilities, she added.

Her arguers saw the downside of possibilities. Three business owners who'd suffered lawsuits in the past wanted protection to try to avoid ever going through that again.

Mary Osborn, with her military upbringing, wanted structure.

Dale Muegenburg, with her legal background, wanted a contract.

"This experiment was supposed to be fun," Jonell insisted. "Do we need a legal contract for a fun deal?"

Others countered, "We live in a litigious society."

To Jonell, the "world's out to get us" approach brought out the worst in people. To her opponents, Jonell's philosophy was naive.

Jonell wanted the group to operate from a place of trust; others believed that "the world isn't always trustworthy."

Verbally adept, Jonell enjoyed debate. The dissension caused others to squirm.

Jonell had her supporters. "Our whole legal system is an antiquated system invented by men," said Roz McGrath. "Women can create something better."

Back and forth the arguments volleyed.

In the midst of the controversy, one woman's voice resonated with both sides. Mary Karrh shared Jonell's sensibilities—she'd been a hippie, too—but throughout her working life, she'd been in business, the last two decades as an accountant. She understood both points of view.

At previous meetings, her soft-spoken words were often drowned under the more strident voices. "Excuse me, can I talk now?" she'd ask, raising her hand. Her ideas were usually unheard until someone else voiced them later. This time, however, the women listened.

"We already are a partnership," she said. "We can form a legal entity in several ways, and an LLC can work well to deal with the business world. We also need some agreement to report our income and expenses for taxes. It's just a formality. But we can have fun with it, create something different. We can still give money to charity."

Mary Karrh had found the right words to appease Jonell. The lull would be short-lived.

VENTURA FINANCIAL PARK is a modern, two-story building with nineteen offices wrapped around a stunning open-roofed atrium. Mary Karrh sits behind her desk at the small accounting firm, which she's owned with a female partner for eighteen years. Tax returns, issues of the *Federal Tax Weekly*, and a calculator rest on her desk. Boxes of client files hug the walls; more client files fill the bookshelves. During tax season, she works fifty to sixty hours a week; in off-season, she works half that number.

Mary is tall and thin, with luxuriantly thick, short hair and a wholesome, pretty face. Freckles splash her face and arms. She wears little makeup, only mascara and blush. "I've always been natural," she says. "It's a lot less work. Fortunately, my husband prefers me this way, too.

"Growing up, I had a hard time making friends. I was a military brat, so we moved around a lot, and I was shy. I was uncomfortable around other girls. I had little interest in clothes or makeup. Most of them wanted to get married. I wanted a career. I had lots of male friends, but I didn't have a close female friend until I was eighteen. Men seemed more interesting.

"I grew up comfortably middle class. As soon as I turned sixteen, I got a job as a cashier on the military base where my father was an air force navigator, and I got my own checking account. Even though there were no scanners then, I knew the price of every item, and at the end of the day, my accounting always balanced to the penny.

"I never had issues with money until I was forty and my father died. He had no life insurance and there were problems with his Social Security benefits. I got this panicky feeling: What if something happened to my husband—he's eight years older than I am—so I made him get life insurance. For the first time in my life, the thought of not having enough money scared me.

"A few years later, I got the same panicky feeling when I thought about retirement. When would I retire? Could I even afford to retire? I took a ten-week seminar on money, where we had to talk about a specific concern. I talked about retirement. What I discovered was that I didn't want to retire. I love what I do. Feeling productive in my work is meaningful to me. It's stimulating to come into the office. I get to work with CEOs and CFOs. Accounting keeps my brain active. Why should I retire just because my friends or husband do or because I turn sixty or sixty-five? I realized retirement wasn't connected to money. That discovery was huge, worth far more than the hundred-dollar cost of the seminar. I rarely talk about retirement now.

"The seminar also encouraged us to change our attitude about money, treat it more as a game than an obstacle. Right at that time, Jonell approached me about the necklace. Buying it seemed outrageously fun—out of the box for me."

THE LLC DISCUSSION yanked Mary back "in the box."

Dale came to the next meeting with a thirty-four-page operating agreement that she and her committee had labored over for weeks. Jonell blanched when she saw it. Mary Karrh flinched. Eye-scanning the document, Mary thought, here's the legal world's version of covering your ass: code sections, protocols, thirty-five definitions, legalese of "whereins" and "heretofores," four pages of tax effects that Mary thought certain she was the only one who could understand. The voluminous document even required signatures of the husbands because of California's property law.

Half the group loved the document on sight. Jonell hated it.

Tensions flared. Voices rose. The debate ceased being fun.

Finally, Jonell lost her patience. "This group was *my* idea," she snapped, "and I don't want this document." Jonell hoped that would end the argument. She'd grown up an only child, which meant eighteen formative years of never having to negotiate with siblings, years of getting her way. She wasn't getting her way now, and she didn't like it.

Among the women were seven firstborns, including Dale, women who'd led their siblings, their classrooms, their businesses. Dale suggested the group go over the document, paragraph by paragraph, "wherein" by "heretofore." Once again, discussion devolved into deadlock.

Once again, Mary Karrh's words emerged as the voice of equanimity and compromise. "This arguing isn't productive," she said. "Let's study the document at home. Some of us would like something simpler, less conventional. I'll volunteer to create a compromise between the verbal agreement Jonell would like and the formal document others want, something everyone can live with. We can discuss it at the next meeting."

Everyone agreed. Then the women defined consensus: Each woman would get her say and every other woman would listen to it. In the end, even if a member disagreed with what the group wanted, she had to let go of her position to align herself with the group—the only way to resolve the issue and move forward.

The experience had exhausted Mary. She was looking forward to Saturday, when she'd head to the golf course, a favorite place to unwind.

Saticoy Country Club is a low-key, unpretentious club whose primary attraction is golf. The challenging 120-acre course, which some golfers whisper is "the best-kept secret in Southern California," winds through avocado groves and agapanthus fields, sycamore and eucalyptus trees, and views of both the Santa Susana Mountains and the Pacific Ocean. Ventura's enviable sunny skies, cool air, and seventy degrees—ordinary weather for Ventura, extraordinary to much of the rest of the continent—make golfing a year-round sport. Today's a club tournament, though Mary plays in spite of it, not because of it. Entering the tournament is the only way she can play golf today. She's wearing knee-length white shorts, a black polo shirt, and a visor with the pink ribbon breast cancer symbol, which is repeated on a pin and a rubber bracelet.

"I think of my life's timeline as Before Cancer and After Cancer," she says while driving an electric cart. "After I was diagnosed—the year I turned fifty-one—I knew everyone would want to know how I was but didn't necessarily want to call me. So many people don't know what to do or say. So I took charge. My husband and I researched the disease and the treatments, and I wrote e-mails about what was happening. So many women asked to be put on my e-mail list that it grew longer and longer. Tamoxifen turned me into a creature I didn't recognize, so those e-mails I wrote were my therapy.

"Comfort doesn't come naturally to my husband. When I was diagnosed he wasn't there for me. He wasn't a shoulder to cry on. He's not affectionate by nature, so I knew it wasn't personal, but when cancer strikes, it is personal, and I took it hard. I turned to my women friends, and I made new ones—they were there for me."

One of the women that Mary's playing with in the tournament walks to the tee box. She swings.

"Great drive," Mary bubbles, then bounds over to the woman to add a hug. "I love your swing," Mary adds, "the way you hold your head so still."

Mary lines up her shot and swings. Her drive lands in the bunker. "Oh, crap!" she moans, then laughs. "When the weather's so beautiful it's hard not to be happy. It's difficult for me to play against friends because I want them to do well, too. I like to play golf because it's a gentleman's game, a game of honor."

Mary tallies the score. She's always the designated scorer, she says, just as she's the designated checker of the restaurant tab. She also keeps the books for the women of Jewelia.

She steers her monologue back to her breast cancer.

"You wonder why you're still here when so many others have died. You feel that your life needs to mean something. I threw myself into fund-raising for breast cancer. Every year I raise over five thousand dollars. I've gotten zero from friends who live in million-dollar homes and five dollars from people on Social Security. Of the nongivers, I always think, 'We have so little time left. Why be selfish?'

"Cancer's given me an opportunity to be a better person. When people die suddenly they can leave a mess. It's a gift to know that you're going to die. Why wait till then to tell people how you feel about them? If I died today, there'd be little unsaid. Generosity isn't just about giving money; it's giving of yourself, your time, your words. Now I hug like I'm never going to let go.

"I used to be very political in the sixties. I marched in Ban the Bomb demonstrations, participated in sit-ins at People's Park in Berkeley—did everything but get arrested. But I lost the passion. I didn't turn into a complete yuppie, but I joined the corporate world, became increasingly apathetic. As a hippie I felt I helped make an impact. That feeling started to come back with the breast cancer fund-raising, now even more with these women. Jonell's passion is contagious. This group has made me feel more involved, more alive. It's made me feel passionate about life again. Of all the investments I've made, the necklace was the best twelve hundred dollars I ever spent."

MARY KARRH DROVE excitedly to the next meeting. She felt good about what she and Jonell and Dr. Roz had achieved: In four hours, they'd pared the document to seven pages, using simple language and making the agreement less restrictive. She'd e-mailed their edited version to the other shareholders. Although she felt a little uneasy that no one had responded, her attitude remained upbeat and hopeful.

As soon as the business part of the meeting got under way, she knew within minutes their simpler agreement wasn't going to fly. The women didn't even want to discuss it. Their dismissiveness disappointed Mary.

It devastated Jonell. She felt both betrayed and abandoned by her friends. Once again she pushed her stance, and once again she hit a wall as hard as the diamonds that had started it all.

Jonell's body stiffened. Her mouth quivered as she tried to hold back tears. Her emotions told her that the time had come to let go. Her intellect told her that if she didn't yield, the group wouldn't survive.

"Do whatever you want," she said. "I'm done."

The LLC marked a turning point: the end of *Jonell's* group and the beginning of *the* group. She'd wanted to see what would happen when thirteen gutsy women got together. Now she saw: Together, they were a force. Together, they outvoted her. From the beginning she'd wanted the group to prove stronger than the individual. She just never imagined she'd be the individual the group would be stronger than. She never imagined that the group's voice would become more powerful than *her* voice.

She signed a document that violated everything she believed, and she stayed upset for months. She never mentioned the LLC again.

The group would move forward and Jonell with it. Once again, the very thing that anguished Jonell would prove the beginning of something wonderful for all thirteen.

CHAPTER NINE

Nancy Huff, the exuberant

. . .

Creating more fun

A FTER THEIR SEVEN-THIRTY A.M., THREE-AND-A-half-mile beach walk, Jonell, Patti, and Dale stopped at Palermo. Nancy Huff usually joined the "Walkie Talkies," as some of the townsfolk called the women, but she had to get to her office early today. This September morning, the diamonds glittered against Jonell's black Lycra tank top. She'd just gotten the necklace—her second go-round with it.

Soured by the aftertaste left by the LLC discussion six weeks ago, Jonell's mind started to spin again. The others could contract the group with legal protections, she thought, but she'd figure out a way to expand what the necklace was all about.

Rosslyn Nikala, the twenty-seven-year-old barista behind the counter, took the women's order of three double lattes and a cheese bagel. Then she noticed the necklace. "I love diamonds," she said, speaking slowly, accentuating each word, prolonging the l-o-v-e. "I have a diamond engagement ring," she went on, displaying her left hand, "diamond earrings, a diamond necklace my husband gave me for our first Valentine's Day after we married, but it has just three diamonds. One day, I want one like yours."

Jonell had seen a lot of women stare at the necklace but

never with such transparent desire. She unhooked the diamonds and reached over the counter to clasp them around
Rosslyn's neck. The gesture was a natural act for a woman
committed to egalitarianism but an unnatural one for the
young woman on the receiving end. Rosslyn's eyes glazed
over. "Oh wow." That's all she could say between sharp, un-
believing breaths. "Wow. Maybe I'll get one like this after
I've been married ten years. God, I hope so. You have made
my day."

Jonell absorbed the words she'd just heard with the bliss
on Rosslyn's face and birthed a grand, new idea.

Outside, where regulars crowded the small, round tables, Jonell offered the necklace to a woman she knew, an
ageless artist. "Would you like to wear the necklace for a
while?" Jonell asked.

"Oh yes! Could I?"

The petite, tanned artist sat there looking as surprised
and giddy as if she'd won the lottery. After fifteen minutes,
Jonell offered it to another, and then another. On this
morning, the regulars were mostly men, but that made no
difference to Jonell. A developer, a sculptor, a salon owner,
a realtor, a musician—they were all game to sport the
stones. Some preened like peacocks. Some strutted. Some
laughed. "I should have worn heels," quipped a strapping
police officer, the diamonds a standout against his navy
blue uniform but an odd accessory to the gold badge. Once
the crowd decided that white T-shirts didn't do justice to
the necklace, two artists good-naturedly stripped. Patti,
with her ever-present Sony Cyber-shot, snapped pictures
of everyone wearing the necklace, while Dale applauded

each pose. The men debated whether the diamonds looked better on hairy chests or smooth ones. Smooth won, 6–0. As they discussed the necklace, the men considered what they might share: a boat, an RV, a Porsche? On this morning, Palermo was the place not just for lattes and the *Los Angeles Times* but also for an unexpected jolt of conversation and community.

Ventura, originally San Buenaventura ("city of good fortune"), began as the last settlement of Father Junipero Serra, the Spanish Franciscan monk who founded the chain of California missions. Once a sleepy little town on California's coast, dubbed by residents Mayberry-by-the-Sea, today Ventura is a thriving, eclectic mix of artists and farmers, entrepreneurs and environmentalists. Neither a playground for the rich, like nearby Monticeto, nor a tourist attraction like Santa Barbara, Ventura is a working-class community. One section of Ventura County, Oxnard Plains, claims one of the richest soils on the planet, giving it the moniker "Strawberry Capital of the World."

A revitalized downtown teems with new restaurants, galleries, boutiques, and day spas. Shops along the palm-tree-lined Main Street range from the bohemian and preppy to the erotic and quaint, generating the same kind of inclusive feeling as the downtowns of Boulder, Colorado, and Asheville, North Carolina. In spite of its new look, there's nary a parking meter to be found.

Jonell strode to her car even more quickly than usual. Seeing others have fun wearing the necklace had boosted her endorphins. Over the next three weeks she asked, "Would you like to try on the necklace?" as often as she said, "Good Morning." She ringed the rocks around her mother, her daughter, her manicurist, her gardener, saleswomen and customers at Chico's, waitresses at Starbucks, a homeless man and woman she'd come to know on her morning jaunts. Most wore the necklace several minutes, a few as long as an hour. By the end of Jonell's month, some eighty people in town had donned the diamonds.

At the next meeting Jonell excitedly told the group where Jewelia had been. When their turns came around, the others followed Jonell's lead, but each with her own style, in her own way.

IN THE MIDDLE OF the Maulhardt Industrial Center, in Ventura's neighboring community of Oxnard, sits the office of the property management company that owns the twelve-building complex. A blue metal facade decorates the concrete exterior. The office itself is industrial bland, with white walls, gray commercial carpeting, and an acoustical tile ceiling. There's nothing ordinary or dull, however, about the woman in charge.

Nancy Maulhardt Huff is the first person you see at the eighteen-foot-long reception desk, an all-purpose space that functions as Nancy's office and that of her fifty-four-year-old, part-time accountant, Noreen. No doors here, just a computer that the two women share. Nancy's cluttered desktop displays: family photos, a banana, a *People* magazine ("for when things get slow," she explains), colored files on her tenants, a stack of mail, and Post-it notes everywhere.

Nancy runs the company. She also picks up the phone, which rings steadily throughout the day.

Being the head honcho and answering the phone all day doesn't feel odd to Nancy, or to those who know her. They'd tell you she's a bundle of contradictions. She's a trust fund baby who grew up in a five-thousand-square-foot home on a golf course, with tennis lessons at a country club and a quarter horse at a neighboring stable, but is as down-to-earth as they come. She was pregnant when she married at twenty, yet the marriage has endured nearly four decades. She's a devout Catholic who enjoys bawdy repartee. During a typical week, Nancy will visit her widowed mother several times and call her twice a day. Nancy will look in on her brother and check his house for gas leaks. She'll handle the finances for her brother, her mother, her marriage, and her business. And, with it all, she arrives at the office every weekday in perennial high spirits.

The phone rings.

"Maulhardt Industrial Center . . . Hello, sweetheart, how are you?"

She looks at her left palm, then listens some more. "Okay . . . love you . . . bye."

"That was my son in San Francisco. I didn't have any reminders for him. I write my to-do list on my hand with a black marker. I'm always writing on my hand. I call it God's Palm Pilot."

The phone rings.

"Sister Jill. How's life, girl? I can't believe you forgot my birthday. . . . Come up and see me. Can you bring your mother? . . . I need you to start praying for Mom. . . . Okay. . . . Love you. . . . Bye."

"Jill was my college roommate. Now she's a nun. Living with me drove her to God."

Mike, a real estate broker in the adjacent office and one of Nancy's twenty tenants, drops in to say hello. "I got a picture of your baby," says Nancy. "Here I introduced you to your wife and I'm mad you didn't name the baby after me. . . . Oh look, you've got new glasses. Don't you look cute? Do I look thinner? That's all I care about. I weigh more now than I ever have. I'm going on the South Beach diet after my birthday."

Nancy talks a lot about her weight, but it's not what you notice. There's a pixieish quality to Nancy, with her short blond hair ("Give me a bedhead," she instructs her hairdresser), her fresh un-made-up face, her quick movements, her constant chatter. "My nickname in high school was 'the mouth,' " she says. You just know that Nancy was one of the popular girls in school, someone you wanted to be around, because life was just plain more fun when Nancy was there.

She's wearing a cap-sleeved brown cashmere sweater ("twenty-eight dollars from Talbots"), wool glen plaid Ralph Lauren slacks ("twenty dollars from Macy's"), brown suede Gabor flats ("more than everything else put together"). She kicks off the flats and pads around the office in polka dot socks ("from Marshalls"). Tortoiseshell reading glasses slide down her nose.

"I used to have a PI as a tenant," Nancy says after Mike leaves. "He came in with great stories. I called him 'my private dick' until my husband made me stop."

Nancy continually looks out the glass front windows to see the action in the parking lot. As soon as she sees someone approach the office she jumps from her chair and walks out the door into the lot to greet them, talking all the way back to her desk.

"Guillermo!" Nancy leaps up to walk toward the door.

"Do you want your car washed?" he asks.

"Yes, I'd like my car washed. Noreen, you want yours washed? It's on me. . . . Hey, Mike, you want your car washed? I'm paying. . . . Wash them all, Guillermo!"

"I like to give him the business," Nancy says after he leaves. "I can give my money to the Catholic Church to pay for some pedophile's sex case or I can give it to a single dad raising two children—hellooooo?"

The phone rings.

"Mom, are you okay?"

Nancy checks her palm—nothing on there to tell her mom.

"Okay, I'll call you later. Love you. . . . Bye."

"Oh, look, a bus! We never see buses in Oxnard."

The phone rings.

"Yes, hi honey. . . . I can't remember what I was going to ask you. . . . Okay. . . . Sure. . . . Gotta go." She hangs up.

"That was Wayne. Last week was our anniversary—thirty-seven years. To celebrate we had sex with Jewelia. It was fun and different. Can wearing it to bed be good for her? I wonder."

"I'd like to try that," says Noreen, who's calculating rent increases.

"Here," says Nancy, transferring the diamonds from her own neck to Noreen's. "Take it home. You've got the cutest husband." Noreen breaks into a wide grin.

The phone rings.

"Lindy, hi. I'm giving you a night with Jewelia for Paul's sixtieth birthday present. I'll bring it to the party Saturday night. Remember, Jewelia never says 'no.' " Nancy hangs up.

"I never turn down my husband," she says. "Many years ago I agreed to let a girl with cancer live with us. Between taking care of her and my kids, I neglected Wayne, and he left for six months. I vowed never to neglect him again. I'm not always in the mood, but eventually I get there.

"I'm probably the only person who's given bush for Bush. I told Wayne, 'I'll make a deal with you. If you vote for Bush I'll give you sexual favors.' I live with a Democrat. What else could I do? Men are distracted by their little brain, as we call it."

The phone rings.

Nancy listens a few minutes. "Your problem, Gary, is that you have ADD. . . . Okay. . . . Okay. . . . Bye."

"I have ADD," she says. "I'm superhyper. I drove my parents crazy."

"I STARTED DRIVING on my dad's ranch in Oxnard when I was eight. When I was thirteen I took my parents' car and drove forty miles to Santa Barbara. In high school I'd tell my parents I was spending the night with a friend, then drive with my girlfriends to Mexico. To me they were adventures, but to my parents they were crimes.

"My mother was a socialite who gave me three coming-out parties. My dad was a commercial developer who groomed my brothers to take over his business. He thought I should stay home and raise kids. When Wayne asked my dad if he could marry me, my dad said, 'No deposit. No return. She can't cook. She can't sew. I don't know what she can do.'

"Is it any wonder I had no self-esteem? When my dad died, everyone, including me, thought my brothers would run the business. But two of my brothers weren't in a position to do that and the one who's the CFO had another business that he ran. So I took charge.

"I didn't think I could do it. I'd been home eighteen years raising three kids. I hadn't finished college. I wasn't computer-savvy. I'd come home from the office feeling sick and overwhelmed and panicked. I'd wake up in the middle of the night in a cold sweat asking myself, 'What am I doing?' I got the help and encouragement I needed from women. My dad's secretary, who was the brains behind the business, taught me everything she knew as she was dying. My sister-in-law showed me how to use QuickBooks on the computer. Noreen here was a lifesaver. Jonell gave me courage I didn't know I had. I couldn't have done it without my women friends."

"I never imagined I'd be running a business like this. The income from my father gave me a comfortable life, but earning the money myself has made me feel smarter and more confident. I wake up every morning and feel good. I think I'm twenty-one. We're our own mirrors now."

NANCY'S HAVING LUNCH with Noreen in the small meeting room across from the reception desk. Nancy sprinkles almonds on her salad, deals Triscuits onto her plate like cards, and sips from a bottle of water.

Nancy's older brother Steve walks in. Steve's a tall, burly guy, as quiet as Nancy is chatty. Without saying a word he heads toward his office.

Nancy calls out to him, "Do you think your wife would like to wear Jewelia for your anniversary?"

He turns around and stares at her.

"Noreen's gonna get laid. Paul Miller's gonna get laid. I'm just looking out for you, Stevie. It's all about you getting lucky."

Steve's expression says that he's used to his sister's lively patter. He goes into his office and shuts the door behind him.

"I work hard on my relationship with my brother," says Nancy, "in part because he has a wife and four daughters I love."

She finishes her salad, then jumps up to make the rounds of her tenants. To a new tenant, she says, "Call me if you need anything. I'm the landlady mom." She assures a woman whose husband recently died, "Don't worry. I won't raise your rent."

Walking back to her office, Nancy talks nonstop. "My brother thinks I should play hardball, but I don't believe in that. My dad thought compassion was the most important thing in business. I attribute everything to my Catholic girls' education. It gave me a sense of humor, and it gave me my morality. People say I remind them of my dad, which makes me feel that I'm in the right place. He was my hero."

At her desk, Nancy answers the phone half a dozen more times.

Steve's wife, Leslie, walks in. "I need the necklace," she says, "since you apparently promised something to my husband."

"Noreen's wearing it tonight. You need to come back tomorrow. But then I have to have it back Saturday. I promised it to Lindy for her husband's sixtieth birthday party."

"MY HUSBAND WILL go to Paul's birthday party because he's a longtime friend," Nancy says later, "but usually Wayne doesn't want to go anywhere. I used to call him Sparky. Now I call him Sparkless. I'm a social animal, but he's not.

"The morning after our wedding, I said to Wayne, 'I'm so excited. We can walk on the beach, go to Mass at a little chapel in Montecito, then brunch at the Biltmore, explore Santa Barbara. We'll have a great day.' Wayne looked at me and said, 'It's the Super Bowl,' and turned on the TV. In tears I ran to a pay phone to call my dad. 'I want to come home!' I cried. And he said, 'You're not coming home. This isn't your last Super Bowl. Get used to it.' I told him to put Mom on the phone and he said, 'No. Wayne's just breaking you in early. This is life.' I was twenty, pregnant, and scared. If this was life, I didn't want it.

"But I was Catholic. I had to make it work. Plus I was madly in love. Once the kids came, I had lots to keep me busy. When they were in school, I was the soccer mom for every team they played on. I sat on the school board. When my youngest graduated from high school, I lost that community. I used to play tennis three times a week with a traveling interclub team, which I loved. But when I started working here, I had to give that up. So I lost that community too. My daughter and I used to do a lot together but then she moved to San Francisco. I feel isolated here in the office—not a lot of people coming and going.

"Wayne's in construction, so he's up at five, in bed at eight. The night of my birthday he had a cold and fell asleep at six-thirty. I bought season tickets to the theater, but by the beginning of the third act he was asleep. As we've gotten older, he wants to be home more; I want to be out more.

"I saw my friends going out with their husbands to plays and concerts and parties while I was sitting home. I became frustrated and angry. I'd made sacrifices for Wayne. It was my family's money that allowed us to have the life we had. I felt he was cheating me out of something I needed.

"I don't like going places by myself. When I do, my mother has fits. I said to her, 'So what am I supposed to do? Divorce him? That would solve the problem.' But it's not a reason to divorce. I love him, more today than ever. He's my best friend. Our businesses are related, so we have lots to talk about. I call him twice a day to ask his advice. He keeps me grounded and sane. The rest of our life together is good. Plus, he doesn't keep me from doing anything fun.

"Either I was going to snap my bands or find a social life. And if I wanted a social life it was my responsibility to get it. With Jewelia, I got what I needed: more girlfriends, more outings, more fun. Fun doesn't just happen. You have to make an effort to create it. After I've had a few hours of fun, I'm much nicer to live with. I never thought about wearing the necklace to go out. Where would I wear it? I have much more fun loaning it to others than wearing it myself. There's always a story in the loan."

—

HERE'S THE ONE Nancy got to hear from her accountant, Noreen. "When I got home from the office, I was excited to show the diamond necklace to my husband," she said. "He wasn't too impressed by it until that's all I had on. It took us back to our early days when sex was a lot more playful, before we settled into a routine. We giggled talking about all the other people who'd worn Jewelia naked. Having the lights on should be part of the rule. How else can you see the sparkles? The next morning, I didn't want to give it back."

In the words of Nancy's husband, Wayne, "Jewelia turned out to be one helluva sex toy."

Jewelia would turn out to be far more than that as the women shared the necklace with those they liked, those they loved. They shared it with granddaughters on their baptismal days, nieces on their graduation days, mothers on their birthdays. They shared it with colleagues and sisters and neighbors and friends, with giggly teens and grown men. Along the way, a string of bling produced little miracles.

At School

DONELLE CLAYPOOL, *fifty-seven, fifth-grade teacher, Our Lady of the Assumption:* "Teaching in a Catholic school, you don't make a good salary, and a diamond necklace is out of my league. So wearing it for a day was a fantasy, like a little girl playing dress-up. I chose my clothes carefully, wore black to set it off. I'm short and heavy, and wearing the necklace made me feel taller and thinner. Not that anyone else would notice, but it was an internal feeling that made me feel good all day. What really felt good was the closeness I felt with Tina when she offered it to me.

"The students were so interested in the necklace story that I asked them what they had of value that they might be willing to share. The necklace spurred a wonderful class discussion on friendship and generosity."

GABI AGUIRRE, *fourteen, eighth grader, Our Lady of the Assumption:* "I got to be the newscaster for our mock trial because that's what I want to be when I grow up. I was practicing and talking really fast and Mrs. Osborne said, 'If you speak slowly I'll let you wear Jewelia.' I was so excited I practiced all night. When Mrs. Osborne put it on me the next day I had a huge boost of self-confidence because I was wearing a million-dollar necklace. It didn't really cost a million dollars but that's what it felt like. My mom took a million pictures of me with it on—well, not a million but a lot—and she framed one for my bedroom. Jewelia's no longer on my neck but she's still there. Mrs. Osborne is one teacher I'll never forget."

MARISSA HOOD, *seventeen, senior, Foothills Tech:* "I asked my mom if I could wear it to school on my sixteenth birthday. It was so cool. I wore it the whole day. I felt I had something to show off, and everyone wanted to see it. What was really cool was that my mom trusted me. She knew I'd be careful."

At Work

CAROL FREEMAN, *forty-nine, letter carrier, U.S. Postal Service:* "I'd heard about the necklace, so I asked Dale about it when I saw her on my route. She said, 'Would you like to wear it?' My uniform didn't do it justice, but what an experience! I've been delivering mail for twenty-two years and I've never had anything happen as cool as that. I felt uplifted the rest of the day. When I got back to the post office, I bragged to everyone about it. How often does a letter carrier get to wear a diamond necklace on her route, or even get to wear one at all?"

ANNA SERRETEC, *thirty-three, warehouse supervisor, Fashion Forms:* "I asked to wear it because diamonds are my birthstone, and having a diamond necklace has been one of my dreams for a long time. All the girls in the warehouse were looking at me like, 'Wow!' I'd been depressed because I'm overweight, but wearing the necklace made me feel happy. More than that, it made me feel exciting. It made me feel sexy."

LUCY WILLIAMS, *fifty-two, stylist and owner of the hair salon Lucy in the Sky:* "I had chills going down my spine. I was actually Lucy in the Sky with diamonds. Before it was 'with zirconium.' Wearing it while I was giving a haircut tickled my innards. Sometimes when I'm in my garden I think back on wearing that diamond necklace. It was such a glorious feeling, like eternal sunshine, a lovely, hopeful feeling for the planet."

ANDREA LEON, *twenty-six, surgical coordinator:* "All of us got to wear it at the office one afternoon. The work didn't feel so hectic that day. I asked one of the other girls to take my picture with Jewelia so I could add it to my profile on My-Space. I majored in feminist studies at UC–Santa Cruz, and seeing these women offer a diamond necklace to those who couldn't afford to buy one was inspiring. I hope to do that with my friends someday."

LORI SHEPHERD, *forty, office technician, State of California, Sacramento:* "I'd just stepped out of the shower at six-thirty in the morning and there was my sister. I couldn't figure out what she was doing there. She said, "Surprise!" and held up the necklace. She gave it to me to wear for the day for my fortieth birthday. I'm reserved and quiet by nature, but I got excited about that. Driving to work I kept looking at it in the rearview mirror. There was a supervisor at work who would never be able to buy such a thing, never even conceive of having something like that on, so I let her wear it, too. She was so ecstatic, I was as excited for her as I was for myself. I love diamonds, but I could never consider buying something like that when we need a new roof or windows. So I may not ever own one, but I'll never forget that one day I wore a diamond necklace."

MONICA SCHILLER, *sixty, senior consultant, Behavior Science Technology, Inc.:* "On my sixtieth birthday I was conducting a training workshop in Ojai. Early in the morning Mary Osborn gave me the diamond necklace for the day. It was such an unexpected and touching way to be honored. In the afternoon, the office gave me a party. They rolled in a wheelchair and handed me a cane and a basket with granny glasses, Depends, denture cream, Preparation H, an oversized pill dispenser, and a blue-haired wig. I thought to myself, 'You can give me all these horrid aging gifts, but the reality is, I'm sitting here wearing a gorgeous diamond necklace feeling young and beautiful.' "

From a Sickbed

SUZANNE STELLA, *fifty-nine, retired librarian, San Francisco:* "Roz insisted that we all wear it when we were out to dinner. I had on a collared sweater and didn't think the necklace would look right with it, but Roz said, 'That's not the point. I want you to wear it to help with your healing.' My days are spent in doctors' offices and hospitals—I'm on dialysis. That evening was such lighthearted fun. I can't say I felt healed after wearing the necklace, but I was moved by Roz's wanting me to wear it. I felt drawn to what it meant, and maybe that's where healing begins."

CHONA PARDO, *fifty-six, full-time mom:* "My mother was in hospice, in constant pain from stomach cancer. She'd been really sad. Patti Channer came and put the necklace around her and gave her a mirror to look at it. My mom smiled and stayed happy the rest of the day. Patti took a picture of her wearing the necklace and then gave copies to me and my sisters and brothers. My mother died a month later. That picture will always be special, because it's the last picture we have of her, and she's smiling."

At Play

TAKA YAMASHITA, *sixty-nine, retired nurse:* "I got to wear the necklace for our golf tournament, and it elevated my whole mood. It helped me play better and brought me luck. We won first place! I love the spirit of the necklace, that it gives whoever wears it a miraculous moment."

BOBBIE BATTEN, *eighty-nine, Jonell's mother:* "I booked the necklace for my three bridge clubs. When I wear it, everyone's looking at me. It makes me feel special. It makes me feel pretty. The second year, I let all the other women wear it, too."

EIGHT WOMEN CLUSTER around two bridge tables at the contemporary Ventura home of Bobbie Batten. The group has been playing together for twenty years, and they take their bridge-playing seriously. In her silk Chinese blouse, Bobbie blends with her home's Asian decor. Her silver hair is exquisitely coiffed, her nails lacquered pale pink, her beautiful face nearly wrinkle-free. ("Merle Norman cold cream every night for fifteen minutes," she says.)

Each woman focuses on the cards before her while awaiting her turn to wear the necklace. "It's just what my outfit needed," says Ruby, seventy-nine, wearing a hot pink striped T-shirt and hot pink sweatshirt jacket.

Jonell transfers the necklace from one woman to another, photographing each with the diamonds.

"I've never had a diamond necklace on," says Margaret, ninety-four. "It feels wonderful. I don't want to take it off."

"I need another picture," says Jean, who doesn't tell her age. "Stand close enough to get the diamonds, but not too close to my face."

"I don't care about a picture," says Tammy when it's her turn. "I just want to wear the necklace."

Jonell leaves to get Chinese carryout for the women: orange chicken, fried rice, lo mein, and green beans with water chestnuts. As the women lunch, their conversation ranges from a book on the CIA and a child who's an FBI agent to life in Argentina, the fires in Catalina, and the new real estate developments in Ventura. They gab about bridge sites on Yahoo! and the best way to navigate the Web to enter international bridge tournaments.

"Who's got the necklace?"

"I'm still wearing it," says Carolyn, eighty-four, in a pink cardigan twin set.

"You've worn it all during lunch," protests one of the others.

"It just belongs on my neck, I guess," says Carolyn. "It's so comfortable. I'm afraid I can't get it off."

Five months later, one of Bobbie's bridge friends composed her annual Christmas letter with the year's highlights. On the center of the page: her picture, wearing Jewelia.

Another day, across town, in the teachers' lounge at Our Lady of the Assumption, thirteen women are eating salads and oranges and drinking Diet Cokes, reminiscing about their experiences wearing Jewelia. So far Tina had loaned it to six teachers, two teachers' aides, one secretary, and one principal.

"I was walking on air, flushed, glowing all day," said one teacher.

"I liked that it was real," said another. "Usually when people compliment me on my jewelry, I have to tell them it's fake."

"I liked the whole princess/tiara feeling," said a young woman with a ponytail.

"I liked that it was an instant breast enhancer," said a svelte blonde. "I also liked that it affirmed I don't need diamonds to be happy."

The women wondered if men could share something. "Maybe," said one teacher, "if it's the right item, like an expensive car or exclusive set of golf clubs. I bet there'd be some men who'd like to pass a woman around."

Jeweler Tom Van Gundy says that if a woman bought a diamond necklace for herself she'd typically wear it twelve to fifteen times a year. From the condition of the clasp, he calculates that this one is worn seven hundred times a year. "The clasp is always the weakest link in any piece of jewelry," he says. "I have to believe that one of these days the necklace will wear itself out." Until that day comes, women all over Ventura have proven the truth of Mark Twain's words uttered decades ago: "Let us not be too particular. It is better to have old second-hand diamonds than none at all."

CHAPTER TEN

Roz Warner, the leader

...

Finding a sisterhood

*D*R. ROZ WARNER WAS PUZZLED BY THE WOMEN IN THE group who just wanted to have fun. What did that mean? Her whole adult life she'd equated fun with escape, and she'd never escaped. She'd never had time. She held a harsh view of escaping because it would have brought disaster to her life.

So naturally she'd said no to buying the necklace. What else could it be but fun? Then one night at Saticoy Country Club, she saw Patti Channer and Mary Karrh sharing the necklace with girl talk and laughter. Dr. Roz and her husband had just moved their joint gynecological practice from the East Coast to Ventura and had joined the club to meet new people. Hearing Patti and Mary's necklace banter in the powder room, she had to admit an attraction. Not to the necklace, which left her lukewarm, but to the feeling of being in a sorority. She realized that to be in this sorority she'd have to buy the pin.

She'd missed her opportunity four decades ago, though she'd been programmed for it. From a professional, Jewish family, she was the oldest of five and the only daughter of a judge and a homemaker. At Shortridge High School in Indianapolis, she'd captained the cheerleaders and paraded in the homecoming court. She was headed for Indiana University and sorority rush.

Then at seventeen she became pregnant.

Unlike most teenage girls, Roz was a doer rather than a dreamer, with her intellect dominating her emotions. She dispassionately weighed her options. She could get an abortion, but, back then in 1962, abortion was illegal and dangerous. She could go away to have the baby, but she couldn't come home and pretend the birth hadn't happened. She could marry her boyfriend and look ahead to a different life. She chose the third path. For Roz, pregnancy wasn't an obstacle, only a change in plan.

So college for Roz didn't include dating and sororities and making lifelong friends, or, for that matter, any friends at all. As she accommodated her husband's schooling and career, she earned her degree piecemeal at seven colleges across the country, while selling Avon during the school year and running a Travelodge motel in the summer—all the while raising a son.

"After five years, I woke up one day and my husband was gone," she says. "He left a note. I was devastated and crying and filled with terror: How was I going to get him back? How could I tell my mom? I went searching for him, begged him to return. When I came back home without him, I looked at myself in the mirror and said, 'Stop this. Now you can have a better life.' In one day I went from feeling abandoned to feeling crazy to feeling hopeful. It would have been amazing if the marriage had lasted. We were just kids.

"He switched careers and went back to school, so he

gave me only one hundred dollars a month in child support, which made for some terrible years.

"I was living in Indiana and working as a high school biology teacher when I fell in love with a pro basketball player, who was black. My high school had a mixed population, so I was familiar with black culture. My father, who was a strong, opinionated man, sent two of my brothers over to tell me I had to stop seeing this guy or people would hurt me and my son. At that time, a mixed couple could not be together in the Midwest. I listened to my brothers, but I wasn't going to have other people tell me what to do. I packed up my Camaro and drove to L.A. with my six-year-old son. I was twenty-four.

"So I became old when I was young.

"I continued that relationship, which practically killed my dad. The only way for him to deal with it was to deny it, so he denied me. My parents disowned me for a very long time. Not financially—I was self-supporting—but emotionally. I called them monthly, but my dad wouldn't talk to me. My mom would talk only a minute or two and then say, 'I'm not supposed to talk to you.' Their decision saddened me, but it didn't crush me.

"Six years after I left Indiana, I went back home when my dad had a heart attack. When I went to see him in the hospital's intensive care unit, he had a second one. The stress of seeing me was too much for him, though thankfully he survived.

"I started medical school when I was thirty-two. My son was in high school, so we went through school together. It was a grueling time. I told him I couldn't be the kind of parent who's always there because medical school was consuming. I got him into a good school that I knew would look after him. He hung out a lot at his best friend's house. My son was very responsible and is today. When I went back to my high school reunion I took him with me. Why not? He was a member of the class, too."

PETITE AND LEAN, Dr. Roz wears her clothes like a uniform: slim black pants, black Privo flats, and, if it's cold, a charcoal fleece jacket. All that changes is the color of her knit shirt: lilac, chartreuse, fuchsia—colors that play up her shoulder-length gray hair. Photographs from the seventies show her in an Afro, looking like a prettier Barbra Streisand in the beginning scenes of *The Way We Were*. Today, Dr. Roz tames her curls with the four-hour Japanese straightening process. She wears rimless glasses and no makeup. She's tucked the diamond necklace inside her purple polo shirt.

She's making her way to the board room at Saticoy Country Club, where she's just stepped down from a two-year presidency but still serves on the board. The position was nothing new for Dr. Roz, who'd been president of her UCLA medical school class four years in a row and led hospital task forces and health care initiatives in Philadelphia. But for the old boys' network at Saticoy, a woman in charge was a first in the club's eighty-year history. Members speak of her in superlatives: "the most amazing woman," "the consummate schmoozer," "really showed people around here that a woman could run things and run them better than ever."

An elderly couple approach her. The man espies the necklace.

"Watch out," he says to Roz, "you're supposed to make love with that on."

"Should I go home with him?" Roz asks his wife.

"No," she answers, "but I'd like to borrow the necklace."

Her husband interrupts. "You two are making me feel like a piece of meat."

The wife reconsiders. "You can borrow him," she says to Roz.

"That wouldn't bother you?"

"No, he's eighty-four."

Roz laughs, then makes her way to the boardroom. Whether men are eighty-four or thirty-four, she knows that one of the first things many of them think about when they see the necklace is the sex guideline.

"How ya doing, sweetheart?" a board member greets her.

She puts her hand on his arm and smiles. "I have the necklace," she says, "and you know what that means."

"Sure do," he answers. "You're going to have sex with the diamonds."

"That's right," she flirts. "You want to come home with me?"

"Will Michael be there?"

"Probably."

"Hello, beautiful," says another.

In a wood-paneled room with a sweeping view of the golf course, Roz sits among eleven tanned, well-heeled men in their fifties and sixties, retired professionals and businessmen, an insurance agent, a geologist, a judge. Some wear khaki shorts and polo shirts straight off the golf course; others are in suits and ties after a day at the office. As the board members dine on penne pasta, a green salad, and chocolate brownies, members report on finances, renovations, upcoming tournaments, all the issues involved in a multimillion-dollar operation. Roz listens attentively but rarely speaks.

After the meeting, she banters with the chefs, the waiters, the club manager—all men. "Let me give you a hug," she says to each one before saying good-bye.

"MY WHOLE LIFE, I've been out of sync with women," she reflects later. "I grew up in a male-dominated family. I've always worked in a man's world. Basically, I didn't like being with women. They were never in my comfort zone. Men were. I think my mother was the same way. I've gotten through every stage of my life without women friends.

"When I did the ob-gyn rotation, I recognized that I could counsel women, make them feel comfortable. Some of that ability came from teaching.

"When I joined this group, I felt I could have dominated it by my opinion. The women had an unnatural respect for me just because I was a physician. But that doesn't make me an authority on everything.

"I am a scientist, and part of being a scientist is making observations without opinions. I'm quiet in the group. I'm always observing and interpreting and collecting data. I'm interested in group dynamics.

"When I was an intern, we had to sum up a case in three

sentences. That was good training to speak concisely. The flip side is that it's hard to hear other people go on and on, and women in this group go on and on. Women in a woman's world function differently from women in a man's world. It takes longer to resolve anything.

"Meetings I have with men are rarely confrontational. Men are primed to solve their conflicts one on one before the meeting. And men can easily dismiss problems; women attach emotions to the process.

"Confrontational meetings were new to me, but I've learned that I'm skilled in dealing with controversy. Early on, I became the buffer, the equalizer to balance Jonell. Unlike her, I've never had an agenda or expectation. Sometimes it's hard to sit through the meetings, but I've learned the value in my ability to listen and help the group move forward. I feel that the group has used my skills.

"And I need the group. Before I came out here my life was all about work. The baby boomer women were the first generation in peacetime to enter the workforce en masse. So we're coming into this stage of our lives with a deficit of friends because we didn't bring them with us. I practiced for eighteen years in Philadelphia and I had not one female friend there I could talk to.

"These women have kept me from feeling alone. On a day I need to talk to someone, I can call about seven or eight of them just to talk. I know they care about me. I'm self-sustaining. I've fought all my battles by myself. But now I have these women to fill me up when I need to be filled up. They have made my life qualitatively better, given me a foundation I didn't have before. What I've learned is that I do need women in my life, and it's important to have them there."

WHAT HAPPENED NEXT surprised Dr. Roz, and she didn't surprise easily.

A Ventura arts leader approached Patti about an upcoming fund-raiser for affordable housing for artists. The event needed items to auction. Did Patti have any ideas? Patti sure did: An Enchanted Evening with the Women of Jewelia and Twelve of Your Friends. Patti had no idea who'd buy such an event, but she was looking forward to finding out. By the end of the evening, two city leaders paid twelve hundred dollars to meet the thirteen necklace women. Within days, they'd invited some of the biggest names in the community to join them.

On the Enchanted Evening, Patti slipped into purple silk paisley pants, a purple crinkled silk shirt, and purple suede clogs. She wanted everything to be perfect at her hillside home, an unpretentious but exquisite California cottage. And everything was. The twenty-six women dined on Italian stuffed mushrooms, smoked salmon and prosciutto, roasted vegetables with seasoned crème fraiche, an array of foreign cheeses, fresh berries, dried fruits, and three decadent cakes. The women sipped champagne and chardonnay and San Pellegrino. Patti circulated the diamond necklace among the guests.

As the sun set, the women gathered on the gray deck, which wrapped around the front of Patti's house. Beyond the orange, lemon, lime, and tangerine trees lay an unobstructed view of the Pacific from Surfer's Point to the Channel Islands. Oil lamps in red mosaic candleholders cast a warm glow.

Dr. Roz, moderating the gathering, asked each woman to say something about herself. The women were leaders in the arts, in business, in nonprofits, in philanthropy. The darker the evening grew, the brighter the accomplishments and the more modest the narratives. The women of Jewelia felt elevated by these phenomenal women around them, each woman offering the best of herself, connecting to the best in the others.

The thirteen women of Jewelia knew that something had begun. They didn't know what exactly, but that didn't matter. All that mattered that magical night was that the necklace had catalyzed a wider circle.

Patti had led the group to the next stage, and, in so doing, she'd found her direction. She'd add these women to her e-mail list, which would deepen the resource pool. Using the diamond necklace as a vehicle, she'd make more connections, gather more women, work together to make a more profound impact in the community.

At the next meeting, Patti proposed to the group another gathering, where the twenty-six women would each invite one or two friends. Two months later, sixty women arrived at the downtown restaurant Hush to network, to talk about what was missing in the community, to explore what they might work on together.

The gatherings had been so easy to accomplish that Patti's head filled with possibilities. Wouldn't it be neat, she proposed at the next meeting, to acknowledge women who are being honored for their contributions to the community, surprise them with the necklace to wear for these high points of their lives?

And so the group did. With elfin smiles, they surprised a philanthropist with a glimmering and shimmering diamond necklace the night she and her husband were honored as Arts Leaders of the Year. "Never had I worn a necklace or anything on my body worth over twenty thousand dollars," said honoree Sandra Laby. "That in itself was pretty amazing. It was such an innovative and gracious way to help me celebrate an evening that was a highlight of my life."

Sandra Laby's delight led the group to similarly bestow the necklace on a bank teller whose gift of a kidney to a co-worker led her to be named Extraordinary Woman of the Year; a teacher celebrated for thirty years of working with special-needs kids; and a publisher named one of the Top Fifty Women in Business in Ventura County.

"The diamond necklace was a big, sparkly hug, a visual sign that the women were behind me and the magazine," said Amy Jones, forty-one, publisher of *VC Life & Style*. "The necklace has become a community totem, so wearing it made me feel all warm inside, as though I were part of a long line of love in town."

CHAPTER ELEVEN

Jone Pence, the designer

. . .

Celebrating second chances

A . . .

S PRISCILLA DROVE TO THE NOVEMBER MEETING, she was looking forward to seeing the women but dreading the tasks facing her afterward. Her son Sean had just announced that his girlfriend and he were getting married in six weeks. The couple had little money; the young woman's family, no resources at all. As the couple discussed wedding plans, Priscilla sensed they were floundering. "Don't worry," she assured them. "I'll take care of everything."

Assuring herself proved more difficult. Boxes were stacked all over her house, still unpacked from the recent move she and her husband, Tom, had made to a small condo. She was hosting her family of thirteen on Thanksgiving day and again Christmas morning. She had to buy gifts for the whole clan—all while working full-time at the jewelry store as they headed toward the busiest time of the year. She was beginning to worry about how she was going to pull off a December 30 wedding.

Seeing the women temporarily quelled her anxiety. She loved the lighthearted repartee. Jonell wrapped up the meeting by asking what she'd typically come to ask: "Anything any of you want to talk about?"

"My son's getting married, and everyone's invited," said

Priscilla, rushing the words. "I'm really excited for them, and Nicole is lovely. But she has no family to help. I'm worried how I'm going to pull off a wedding for two hundred people on a shoestring—and before New Year's."

Patti, the go-to girl, spoke first. "Okay, everyone, how are we going to help?"

One by one, the women volunteered. Jone Pence, an interior designer, offered to design the space in the church reception hall. Patti volunteered to decorate and coordinate the e-mail correspondence. Tina wanted to bring candles and hurricane lamps from school. Mary Osborn was happy to take off work early the Friday before, and they'd all come early to help the day of the wedding.

Priscilla couldn't speak. She'd just wanted to unburden herself because she knew that, by talking it over, she'd feel better afterward. She'd never expected what followed. Driving home, she started to cry. No one had ever stepped up like that for her. Not once.

THE WEDDING WAS two weeks away, but Priscilla still hadn't bought a dress. She hated to shop. Being pear-shaped meant nothing ever fit; everything had to be altered. She usually headed to Macy's at the mall across the street from her office. The avalanche of choices inevitably inundated her. She could spend hours trying on clothes only to come home empty-handed. Naturally, she'd procrastinated.

Patti got wind of Priscilla's predicament. Patti knew just the store for Priscilla. That was easy—Patti had been in all of them. "Yon Hui's, a boutique on East Main," she said to Priscilla. "I'll meet you there."

When Patti arrived, Priscilla was looking at something blue. No, thought Patti, all wrong for her. Aloud she said graciously, "I don't know about that one." Patti fingered quickly through the dresses, sliding their hangers on the rod, *zip, zip, zip.* She pulled out a champagne-colored two-piece dress with a three-quarter-length lace jacket, to elongate Priscilla's body, with little beads faceted to catch the light. Patti tilted her head, drumming her finger on her cheek. "I like this one better," she said. "This'll be great on you. It's beautiful. It's versatile. You can wear the top with black pants or jeans, the skirt with a black top. Try this one on."

Priscilla glided toward the dressing room, thinking how different this shopping expedition was from past ones. Priscilla had never shopped with a friend before. Patti was so quick, yet, oddly, Priscilla didn't feel rushed.

Priscilla slipped into the dress. It fit! No question, the color accentuated her olive skin and auburn hair.

She came out of the dressing room. The look on Patti's face told her this was the dress.

"That is gorgeous," said Patti. "You look stunning. How does it feel? Is it comfortable? Turn around."

Priscilla turned around. Now she was smiling too.

"Don't buy any accessories," said Patti. "I have everything you need, even shoes, since we're the same size." Patti smiled, which made her eyes glisten.

Priscilla drove back to her office elated. She had her dress—a major task completed—and in how much time? Twenty minutes? With Patti, shopping was not only easy, it was fun. In the past, Priscilla had always thought that the smarter and more successful you were, the more you didn't need other people, the more you could do it all yourself. Priscilla had never asked anyone for anything. Now she was starting to think differently. Maybe the smarter you were, the sooner you recognized you were in trouble and asked for help.

THE DAY BEFORE the wedding, Patti arrived at one P.M. to help set up the reception hall. Priscilla was already there. So was Jone Pence.

New to the group, Jone (pronounced Joanie) had joined when one of the women moved out of town. Jone had been to only six meetings, which meant that she was still feeling her way, still more an observer than a participant.

Jone had been a friend of Jonell's for years but didn't know most of the others. She did, however, know how to transform a space. Jone's naturally raspy voice, blond hair, and bubbly nature give her the kind of girl-next-door, sexy appeal that Doris Day had personified in the fifties. Jone dressed like a designer: She wore neutrals but always splashed on color with an artfully draped red scarf or chic chartreuse sandals. She tooled around town in a cream VW Beetle convertible with her Shih Tzu poodle, Blue, at her side.

Jone loved solving design problems. That's what she did six days a week for some twenty clients she juggled at a time. She also solved problems for millions of viewers of HGTV's *Designers' Challenge*. She'd quickly become the group's resident designer, selecting the colors for fund-raising flyers and signs. She enjoyed hearing the women say, "Jone's here, she'll take care of it."

At the Sacred Heart Church, with the help of Patti and the others, she did. She designed the hall centered by a dance floor—the bride's major request. Jone found twenty round tables in the storage room, which she arranged to allow for ample walking space among them. She created one long table for the wedding party; display tables for the gifts and the tiers of cupcakes that defined the wedding cake; zones for the appetizers and buffet; and an open bar in an adjacent side room. She decided that the poinsettias in the church still vibrant from the Christmas services looked best when lined up like red Rockettes across the foot of the stage. She stationed the church's most attractive trash cans in discreet corners. Finally, she discovered that the recessed lights could be dimmed—unusual for a church, thought Jone, but the element that could transform any space into something special. If you can dim the lights, you can create an atmosphere.

Jone and the Jewelia Wedding Planners dressed the tables with beige and white linens and white votive candles. By five P.M., the space was as pretty as a parish hall could be.

"I ALWAYS LOVED DESIGN," says Jone. "Growing up in Minnesota, when I'd go out in the snow, I wouldn't make snowmen; I'd make houses. I never wanted dolls. I wanted a new canopy bed with matching furniture.

"My parents never talked to me about a career. My mother thought I should go to college to find a husband. At

Cal State–Northridge, I studied to be a teacher for the deaf, but when I fell in love and got married, my life became all about him. He wanted to form a TV production company so I forgot about teaching and ran the business side of the firm—scheduling, ordering, budgeting, finances. I had business smarts. He didn't.

"Our first apartment was a large warehouse in Hollywood. The business was there, too. I hated Hollywood, and I hated the apartment. He decorated it. The loft bedroom was like a sex den, with a fireplace, a gigantic waterbed, bearskin rugs beneath a bear claw tub, and a swing hanging from the ceiling. We had to shimmy down a pole like fire-fighters to get to the ground floor.

"I rented an apartment in Burbank so we could have a marriage away from the business. He never showed up. That was a sign that he wasn't marriage material, but I wanted the marriage to work. I had no game plan after that. I'd internalized the message of my mother's generation: Once you get married, you're complete.

"I was such an accommodating person that I said 'sure' to whatever he wanted. But when you're that accommodating, your partner walks all over you. He was a womanizer, who started cheating on me six months after the wedding. He was always out shooting videos, partying, staying out all night. Once I was in bed sleeping when I heard him in the Jacuzzi giggling with some girl. And yet I was still hopeful. I'm a smart businesswoman, but I'm very slow when it comes to men.

"I wanted a house so badly. My parents helped us buy land on which to build our dream home. The problem was, there was nothing on which to build the marriage. In the five years we were together, he was involved with at least three women.

"One day I balanced the company books, packed my suitcase, and left. I'm sure he had a date that night. They say you go through three major crises in your life: losing your job, your home, and your marriage. I lost all three in one day.

"When I told my mother we were separated, her first response was that I probably didn't cook good enough meals, didn't coordinate the color of the vegetables.

"I moved to San Francisco where I worked for J. Walter Thompson, the ad agency. After five years I wanted a smaller community, so I came back to Ventura, where my parents had moved when I was in junior high.

"Four years ago—I was fifty-two—I bought my first home. It was a mess: dark paneling everywhere, a spray-on acoustical ceiling, a kitchen jutting out into the living room. I gutted it and rehabbed it in three months. I make decisions fast, more like a man, but my house is pretty 'girly' with toile drapes and lots of flowers in the garden. I've finally created this perfect space for myself—my little dream. After I hung my last painting, I danced around the living room for a month to Nora Jones's singing. Paying for the house and designing it all myself felt like a huge achievement.

"I've been divorced twenty years now. I've had many serious relationships, but my marriage was so brutal that I'm gun-shy. Plus I rarely get lonely. I enjoy my own company, and I love having my own space. I do miss the sex and intimacy of a relationship, but it'd be hard for a man to move into my house. His stuff would be a problem. All I could give him now is a sock drawer. But I do love to remodel. I'd happily add on.

"Just in the last ten years my mother has stopped telling me I should have a man. For the last five years of my father's life his health was failing, and he was bedridden for six months before he died. My mother confided one day, 'It's been hard living with your dad.' She finally saw the other side of being married. 'See, Mom,' I said, 'my life's easy.' And she said, 'Jone, you're doing fine on your own. I'm proud of you and your accomplishments.'

"When she finally let go of her dream for me, I felt she saw me for the first time. The struggle was over. We became both friends and confidantes. Finally, everything in my life was comfortable.

"I don't need a man to survive. Everything I have, I earned myself. But I do need my family and girlfriends to survive. When Jonell first called, the time wasn't right. I'd put all my money into renovations and was deep into nesting. I didn't want to go anywhere. What'd I want with a diamond necklace? I'd never had a diamond of any kind.

"The second time Jonell asked, I said yes. One thing I've learned is that life is full of second chances."

THE DAY OF THE Van Gundy wedding, Jone met clients in the morning, then drove straight to the reception hall to make sure everything was in order. The Jewelia Wedding Planners exited early from the ceremony to join her. They lit the votive candles, set out the wineglasses, checked on the food: appetizer trays of salsa and chips, raw veggies and artichoke dip, garlic rolls, and fresh fruit. A Mexican feast of *barbacoa, arroz, frijoles de la olla,* and *bolillos.*

Guests poured into the hall, claiming seats by laying their jackets and purses on the stackable chairs. When more people showed up than had R.S.V.P.'d, Priscilla panicked. Patti put her hand on Priscilla's arm. "Don't worry, doll," she said. "We'll handle it."

Patti nabbed two of the women to set up another table.

Patti scanned the room. Oh my god, she thought, one bartender but no waiters for 150 people! Patti acted fast. She instructed the bridal party to tote the champagne to all the tables, to introduce themselves to the guests—and to make it quick. Chop, chop!

The women of Jewelia, all seated at the same table, felt like a collective fairy godmother as they watched the bride circulate among the tables. With her long white strapless gown and their diamond necklace, Nicole sparkled like Cinderella. Yes, the diamonds had adorned a lot of attractive necks, but none more beautiful than Nicole's. The women devoured the food, which they all agreed was *delicioso.* Patti scanned the room again. She didn't see anyone to clear the tables. My god, she thought, guests at a wedding can't clear their own friggin' plates!

"Okay, ladies, time to clear," Patti commanded, rising from her seat. "Spread out and start bussing."

As fast as she could snap her fingers, the women became waitresses, each taking one section of the room. Priscilla paled when she saw the women clearing the tables. Her color returned when she saw them smiling as they worked. She smiled, too. She relaxed. She breathed.

Priscilla needed to breathe. She was about to sing pub-licly for the first time in a decade. She knew she looked good—she'd never had so many women compliment her on a dress. She was confident of her voice, but she was terri-fied of forgetting the lyrics.

She walked onto the stage. Ten mariachis followed. Her son Sean looked up in amazement. When he had asked her to sing at his wedding weeks ago, she'd said no. He had not understood why she couldn't do this one thing for him. She was always saying no. When he was growing up, she was the family enforcer, the bad cop. At family reunions watching his mom sing, he'd seen her other side. He loved that mom, with the voice and the stage presence. He'd always associ-ated her singing with good times.

Guitars, violins, and trumpets accompanied Priscilla as she sang the Spanish love ballad "Sabor A Mí." Her voice was alto-deep and resonant like a cello, her powerful pipes developed from childhood singing mikeless with a mari-achi band. The women of Jewelia couldn't believe what they were hearing. Priscilla with a voice like that? She sang like a Mexican Edith Piaf, emotionally, with her whole body. Most of the group didn't know the Spanish words, but from the way Priscilla sang, they didn't need to. By the time she'd sung the last note, not a woman in the room had dry eyes.

One man was crying, too: Priscilla's son Sean, the object of her affection. His mom had lent Nicole—his wife!—the diamond necklace to wear. With her friends, she'd done all the work for the wedding. And now with her singing, she'd given him the best gift of all.

When Priscilla's older son, Aaron, a professional deejay,

spun Earth, Wind & Fire's "Let's Groove," the women of Jewelia stormed the dance floor to begin the party. One of the mariachis grabbed Tina. Priscilla and Patti and Nancy danced with one another. Priscilla's face radiated with her successes. She'd pulled off the wedding. She'd pulled off her singing. And she'd made her son happy. She was utterly in the moment, enjoying this day, this music, these women.

"IT WAS MY FIRST social outing with the women of Jewelia," designer Jone said after the wedding. "I thought, 'Oh my god, we're clearing tables.' But it was a big moment for me, seeing the women rise to the occasion to take care of Priscilla, seeing a group of thirteen working as one. My mother belonged to many women's groups, and when my dad became ill, her friends came daily to comfort and support her. I saw what those visits did for my mom, and I realized that I didn't have that in my life. I'd never belonged to a women's group. Seeing everyone come together for Priscilla's wedding comforted me to know that, down the road, a group of women would be there for me."

SIX P.M., FRIDAY, one month after the wedding, Priscilla's taking her third voice lesson. She's standing by a small, upright piano in the living room of her teacher, Toni Janotta. The room is the bohemian, eclectic space of an artist, with colorful mobiles, stained-glass lamps, and a five-foot-tall carpeted scratching post for the Russian Blue cat slinking across the wood floor.

Priscilla's wearing a jungle print top with multicolored spangles and chocolate brown slacks. Toni begins the exercises. Priscilla vocalizes the scales. She sings them breathing deeply from her diaphragm. She sings them widening her range. She sings them in short, staccato sounds that crunch her stomach. She sings them—over and over.

She struggles. She sweats. She perseveres.

Finally, the fun part: Toni leafs through *The Great American Songbook* to select a number in Priscilla's key. She hands Priscilla the book open to a Sinatra classic. Priscilla puts on her tortoiseshell-rimmed reading glasses. She looks down at the sheet music and begins softly:

Out of the tree of life I just picked me a plum
You came along and everything started to hum
Still it's a real good bet the best is yet to come

By the third verse she's belting out the lyrics. She's already absorbed the message.

PRISCILLA IS TIRED and hoarse but energized. She climbs into her silver Mercedes, "my first luxury car," driving with her left hand as the right one constantly gestures. She wants to start auditioning, be in a musical, do community theater. First, though, she has this dream: to perform a cabaret for friends and family. She's set a deadline: two years. She'll rent a restaurant or lounge, hire musicians. select a theme, and then perform her repertoire one or two nights. She'll hire her vocal coach, who's a professional singer, to advise her. Priscilla's excited just thinking about it: An Evening with Priscilla.

"Growing up, I knew I had a gift," she says. "But after I

married and had children I didn't use it. I let it all go. But sharing your voice is a way to connect to people. I'm determined to have a singing career before I die. It's not too late. Without this group of women I wouldn't have imagined it. Now I have friends who will support me in doing something risky. I know they'll be there, and they'll encourage all their friends to be there, too. They'll fill the room.

"Before meeting these women, I lived in a world where I wasn't worthy, wasn't good enough. It's the story I'd told myself all my life. These women taught me that it was just a story, a story I'd told myself because I was afraid. My only fear now is that I'll be a disappointment to myself, that I'll get to the end of my life and know I didn't take advantage of everything that was given to me.

"Before Jewelia, I thought, 'I wonder what'll happen to me?' Now I think, 'I wonder what I'll do next?' For the first time, I'm composing my life."

CHAPTER TWELVE

Mary O'Connor, the rock 'n' roller

...

Shaping a legacy for our daughters / ourselves

*P*ATTI WAS SO MOVED BY THE SIGHT OF PRISCILLA'S daughter-in-law in the diamonds that she offered the necklace to a friend's daughter for her upcoming wedding. Patti didn't have a daughter, but she doted on those of her friends. She was a godmother to ten, including this bride-to-be, who'd grown up with some of the Jewelia women's daughters. The news that her "something borrowed" would be Jewelia spread quickly through Ventura.

Some of the Jewelia women's daughters were surprised, one miffed, one frankly "bummed out" that an outsider to the group would be wearing the necklace on *her* wedding day before they'd be wearing it on *their* wedding days. The mothers groused. That their daughters could wear Jewelia on their wedding days had been one of the reasons they'd bought the necklace in the first place. They didn't like this turn of events.

And they didn't like hearing about the loan through the grapevine. Shouldn't they have been consulted? Whoa, shouldn't there have been a discussion? The wedding wasn't even during Patti's month. She borrowed the necklace to loan it to a third party. Is this the way the women were going to operate?

The chain that bound them chafed once again. And once again, all hell broke loose.

AT THE NEXT MEETING, Patti opened with an apology. Her intention had been only to share, she said. Isn't that what the group was all about? Isn't that what they'd been doing for a year now?

Well, yes, that was what they were all about, said Nancy Huff. But *weddings* were different. Weddings were sacred events that blessed and honored family life. The necklace was to be a family heirloom bestowed on *their* daughters for *their* wedding days. There's a difference between loaning it to someone for a few hours at work, she said, and loaning it to someone for a *wedding*.

Patti looked at Nancy incredulously. Could this be the same generous, compassionate Nancy she'd known for twenty years? What happened to her?

"There's no difference," Jonell responded. "Sharing is sharing."

"Something that is common and easily available loses its value," opined another mother of a marriageable-age daughter. "If anyone can wear it for her wedding, then it won't be special for *our* daughters."

"No," declared Jonell. "What makes the necklace special *is* the sharing."

"I think we should go back to sharing the necklace just among the thirteen of us, the way it was at the beginning," said a third mother of a marriageable-age daughter.

"You've got to be kidding!" Jonell exclaimed. "What's happening to this group? What are we all about anyway?

The only interesting thing about this experiment *is* the sharing."

"Yes, we're about sharing," someone answered, "but we've never talked about *how* we'd share. Maybe we need to set up some guidelines."

Guidelines? Jonell was aghast. *Not this again.*

"We just want to preserve the specialness of the necklace for our daughters. I don't want my daughter to not want to wear the necklace because so many others have worn it before her."

"You're forgetting the basic premise of this experiment," Jonell reminded them. "It's about inclusion, not exclusion."

Jonell, too, had a daughter of marriageable age but no affinity for this point of view.

"At the least," interjected another mother of a twentysomething daughter, "we should discuss loans for weddings and other public events ahead of time, reach a consensus."

Jonell lost her patience. "You're telling me that I have to go through some committee before I can share this necklace with someone?"

To Jonell, this argument was worse than the one over the LLC. This controversy went to the heart of her experiment. She'd shared it with the twelve of them. How dare they not share it with others?

"This was *my* idea, and the necklace is for *everyone*," she flared. "There are *no* constraints."

The room grew very quiet.

Finally Nancy, Jonell's oldest friend in the group, spoke.

"Yes it was your idea, Jonell. But the necklace isn't just about you anymore. We're a group now."

"You're right," Jonell acceded. "I'm sorry."

Half the group said nothing. Those without children couldn't even wrap their heads around the discussion. Those who'd survived major illnesses couldn't sit still for it.

The woman who broke the silence said the necklace should *mean* something to the wearer. Maybe those who wear Jewelia to public events, like weddings, should do something in her name, like give money to charity.

Jonell finally erupted. "Now you're saying that women have to *pay* to wear the necklace?"

Emotions surged and spilled and exploded. By the end of the evening, the women had resolved nothing.

Nancy went home upset. She felt like quitting the group. Jonell went home upset. She wished she'd never started it.

NO ONE HAD listened to the debate with more interest than Mary O'Connor.

Mary was one of the few who'd written a check for the necklace without seeing it. She didn't need to. The lure had been one thing, and one thing only: She wanted the necklace in order to lend it to her daughter Karen on her wedding day. Mary reasoned that, after she died, Karen, as her beneficiary, would come to know—and become friends with—the daughters of her friends.

When December rolled around and with it her annual time with the necklace, Mary O'Connor turned the meeting into a party with the legacies. December was the perfect time to host a party, though Mary didn't need an excuse.

At sixty-two, Mary O'Connor was the oldest member of the group, but she still partied and dressed like a rock star. She wore snug, pastel leather jackets, cleavage-revealing camisoles, mid-thigh skirts. A delicate, gold ankle bracelet circled a smooth, bare leg. Blond waves cascaded past her shoulders. Her look was not typical for a former chair of a high school English department, but hers was a look that helped make her the groovy teacher all the kids wanted to have.

She still joined the crush at six rock concerts a year with her second husband, a space systems engineer ten years her junior. She'd taken her two kids to their first rock concerts, shared a love of Led Zeppelin with her son; Hall & Oates with her daughter. The couple's partying habits were rooted in their early years in Buffalo, New York, when they'd pick up their babysitter at eleven-thirty P.M., hit the bars and clubs until four A.M., grab some breakfast, and head home. Now that their children were adults, Mary and her husband were invited to parties hosted not only by their children but also by their children's friends. The couples' youthful spirit made them A-list invitees.

Mary O'Connor liked to throw a party as much as she liked to attend one. For her evening to cede the diamonds, she went all out decorating her five-level Spanish-style home. She festooned the stair railings with pine garlands, interspersing the greenery with twinkling lights and ribbon bows in burgundy and gold. She hung three evergreen wreaths, decorated a twelve-foot-tall Noble pine, and strung lights across her three-tiered deck overlooking the Pacific. Everyone, as usual, congregated around the buffet in the dining room. Potluck had reigned at previous meetings, but Mary supplied all the holiday fare herself: jumbo shrimp, salmon and crab dips, assorted croissant sandwiches, and tamales, a Southern California holiday staple.

The women arrived with their beneficiaries—daughters, stepdaughters, nieces, and sisters. Seated around the living room, with half the women sprawled on the floor, Mary had so much fun hosting the generations that at the end of the evening she spontaneously invited the women of Jewelia to her home in the Florida Keys. No one in the group had ever seen Key West, but no one was surprised that the party girl had a second home twenty miles from one of the country's great party towns.

"First seven who get plane tickets can come," she said with cheerleader enthusiasm. Three months later, in her floral halter tops and white shorts, Mary introduced the women to the best conch fritters and *mojitos* on the island. She took them to every legendary bar: Sloppy Joe's, Captain Tony's, the Hog's Breath Saloon, and her favorite, the Green Parrot. She led the caravan to tour the Hemingway Home and Museum, cruise the shops on Duval Street, and watch the sunset at Mallory Square. Each night, Nancy and Tina, usually in bed by ten P.M., would start yawning and ask, "Can we go home?" Mary's response: "But it's only two A.M.!"

Back home in Ventura, Mary's daughter, Karen, couldn't keep up with her, either.

A younger version of her mother, Karen has Christie Brinkley looks: an animated, pretty face and a curvy, athletic body. Like her mother, she's an emphatic speaker and gesturer. The two women work together at Mary's computerized sign business. Together they attend church, the LA Opera, and the Super Bowl when they can snag tickets. They're avid sports fans and best friends.

"When I first heard about the necklace, I trivialized it," says Karen, thirty-nine. "When my mom told me I could wear it on my wedding day, I thought, 'Yeah, right. That'd be nice, but it'll never happen.' I've never been married and thought every other woman's daughter will wear it before I will. But the first time I saw my mother wear the necklace, to a family Christmas party, it changed everything. The necklace was so beautiful, and she just glowed. I think it's because of what the necklace means to her, it's like wearing your heart on your sleeve, although in this case it's her neck. I thought, 'That'll be so beautiful to wear on my wedding day.'

"But now, if everyone in town's gonna get to wear it, it doesn't feel special anymore. I'd rather wear my grandmother's pearls."

Mary O'Connor didn't care that another young woman would be wearing the diamond necklace before her daughter. She cared about only one thing: Her daughter wasn't as excited about wearing it as she once was.

MARY ANN O'CONNOR was raised in an upper-middle-class family in Williamsville, New York, a suburb of Buffalo. Her father was a radiologist; her mother, an Irish beauty who promenaded in the grocery store in high heels and a mink. As the oldest of four and the only daughter, Mary often babysat for her younger brothers. Her household was a male-dominated one.

"I was a good student, good athlete, class leader, and captain of the cheerleaders, but my parents seldom came to my school functions. They were too busy raising my brothers. I rarely got my mother's attention. When I was a senior in high school, I thought, 'Maybe now,' but then she became pregnant again. I remember the one time she came to see me cheer. She'd brought my younger brother along. I was thrilled to see her in the stands. Ten minutes later, after finishing a routine, I looked up to see her leaving. Later she told me my brother had threatened that if they didn't leave the gymnasium he'd scream his head off. At the time, not getting more of her attention was hard. Plus, I would have liked to show her off. She was very glamorous.

"My situation was very different with my own daughter. She was my only child for twelve years. Four of those, I was a single parent, so it was just the two of us, and we bonded. I taught in schools where she was enrolled. When she made cheerleader, I coached the squad. When she was a sports reporter, I moderated the school paper. I chaperoned her proms. I endured three hours of Duran Duran—not my favorite music—so that she and three friends could go to the group's concert in L.A.

"I was just as involved with my son. I was always his team mother, saw every game. When he was in high school playing football, I dropped everything to help his team's preseason "Hell Week," where the players practiced, ate, and slept at school for five days. I actually took vacation time to help out. I hauled water and Gatorade and oranges to the field. I made big pans of lasagna and huge pasta salads for sixty-five boys. I served their lunches and dinners, cleared the tables, and loaded the dishwashers.

"The players were supposed to bring mattresses from home in order to sleep on site. I noticed that my son's mattress was still in our truck, so even though he was a six-foot, 190-pound kid in prime physical condition, I decided to lug his mattress to the sleeping room for him. I was wrestling with this extra-long mattress, dragging it on the ground, when a couple of coaches walked by me. I heard one say to the other, 'Do you think she's going to come back tonight to tuck him in?' I was so embarrassed. When my son saw what I was doing he was mortified. He grabbed the mattress, and I slunk away. That's when I realized I was a helicopter mom.

"The pattern was so entrenched, though, that I couldn't throttle the engine.

"When my daughter wanted a house, I took time off from work and spent my weekends helping her house-hunt. Practically every day for three months I inspected the house with her as it was being built, went over every detail. I helped her select tile and flooring and fabrics and furniture. I helped her move in and unpack and hang draperies. I designed her backyard.

"I've really missed teaching. I never expected to stay with the sign business more than a few years. I think of Pink Floyd's lyrics from *The Dark Side of the Moon:* 'And then one day you find / ten years have got behind you.' I've stayed with the business because it's enabled Karen and me to work together.

"I've worked all my adult life, as a teacher and a business

owner, but my primary identity has been as a mother. If my kids need me for anything, everything else fades away. I still help both my kids with their finances. I suffer through my daughter's relationships. Chrissie Hynde sang, 'Take me into your darkest hour and I'll never desert you / I'll stand by you.' That's the way I feel as a mother.

"I realize that my hovering is a weakness. I see now that in raising me the way she did, my mother gave me a great gift: independence. I was more independent at twenty-one than either of my children were. What I've also come to realize is that the more you hover over your children, the more empty the nest when they leave. And children have to leave.

"My son took a job promotion and moved to Nevada—the first time in twenty-eight years he's lived more than thirty minutes away. My daughter just started a new job—the first time in twenty years we haven't worked together. It's been a huge adjustment. Detaching is hard. I miss them.

"Growing up, I had a wonderful group of girlfriends from second grade through high school. The nuns dubbed us 'The Fast Fifteen.' We shared clothes, confidences, crises, laughs. When my mother was preoccupied with my brothers, I turned to these girls. Forty years later, we've stayed connected and get together every year.

"Now with Jewelia I have a wonderful new group of women friends. I've joined the morning walkers. Nancy Huff and I bought season theater tickets together. Having these women in my life fills a tremendous void. I once thought my husband and I would retire to the Florida Keys, but I don't think that anymore. I don't want to leave these women."

IN THE AFTERMATH of the sharing brawl, Mary O'Connor, like the English teacher she once was, cared only that the sharing was *defined*. Nancy Huff, meanwhile, turned to a woman she respected and whose opinion she valued: her daughter Christen, a twenty-seven-year-old nursing student. "Are we being selfish?" she asked her plaintively.

Christen's first response to the wedding loan, like those of some of the other daughters, had been irritation. Her irritation, however, lasted only thirty minutes; it was much shorter-lived than her mother's. Christen answered her mother bluntly. "I think you're losing sight of what's important," she said. "It sounds to me like you mothers are having a 'high school' moment. It doesn't matter to me who wears the necklace. I still want to wear it on my wedding day and when I have my first child. I want to wear it for the significant moments of my life."

Christen suggested a journal so that women who wear the necklace to public events, like weddings, could write what the experience meant to them. A journal would grant the necklace not only a history but also a soul.

Amid a flurry of e-apologies, Nancy e-mailed the group Christen's idea, which the women unanimously loved. Christen Huff had not only helped resolve the controversy, she did so with such creativity and graciousness that she assured the women that their legacy of sharing would continue into the next generation.

The next day, at the gift shop in Palermo, Patti skated through the wares, *zip, zip, zip.* She found a portfolio-style soft leather journal with an Asian-influenced floral filigree design, colors of gold and red and green blooming onto a black background—the perfect accessory for Jewelia.

CHAPTER THIRTEEN

Roz McGrath, the feminist

. . .

Raising awareness of women's lives

*T*HE CONTROVERSY OVER SHARING HAD TAKEN A TOLL on Jonell. Something's gotta give, she decided, and that something was running the meetings. She was too talkative, too opinionated, too forceful. Her dominance inevitably provoked opposition.

"You wear it, you chair it," Jonell announced at the next meeting.

"Great idea!" said one woman after another. Jonell laughed to herself. Wonder how long they'd been wishing for that? Roz McGrath was next in line to wear the necklace so she'd be the first to implement the new idea. Roz looked forward to leading the group. She'd come up with a fun project. As one of the three childless women in the group, she couldn't listen to the "sharing" debate. She left the meeting early and didn't read the subsequent e-mails. She didn't have time for such nonsense. She was overwhelmed by commitments, the first of which was selling her produce at the farmer's market. She had work to do.

SATURDAY MORNING, AT eight A.M., Roz pulls up to the market in old town Camarillo in her beat-up '76 Chevy pickup, imprinted with the sign ORGANICALLY GROWN MCGRATH FAMILY FARM.

Roz ties a purple apron over her pale blue camisole and short khaki skirt. She's freckled and petite, with dark brown hair and eyes. She looks a little like Stockard Channing, who combines a soft face with tough roles. Roz embodies a dichotomy, too: both gentle and genteel in her demeanor, but rugged in the dirt and rabid in her politics.

Divorced for eleven years, retired from teaching for four, she co-manages the family farm, selling its crops at eight markets from Ojai to Santa Monica. The business also supplies organic produce to some thirty high-end restaurants in Santa Monica, Malibu, and Beverly Hills.

A fifty-eight-year-old blond hunk, a commercial diver and her new love, helps arrange the vegetables in appealing groupings. On the canopied display space burst an array of color and texture: French green beans, Italian ferono beets, miniature Asian corn, plump carrots, curly red-leaf lettuce, baby greens, black radishes, green onions, parsnips, chard, and strawberries. Lots and lots of strawberries.

"I like beets the most," Roz says. "I boil them until I can poke a fork through, then slice them and serve with gorgonzola and walnuts."

To the side of the main table, Roz groups bouquets of lilac caspia, golden yarrow, Indian red straw flowers, artichoke flowers, and sunflowers.

"Just put a little hairspray on the caspia and it'll last longer," Roz advises a buyer.

An elderly man approaches to buy beans and carrots. "Thanks, young lady," he says.

Roz smiles at him. "You're welcome."

When he's safely out of hearing, Roz says, "I hate it when people call me young lady. I'm not young, and I'm not a lady. I'm a woman and an older woman. So don't call me that. And don't mess with me." She smiles a knowing smile. She knows that people will continue to call her that, and she knows that she'll continue to be irritated.

A sixtyish woman, who's selling at a neighboring stall and who's decked out in a large flowered hat, waves to Roz, then sees something that catches her eye. She walks over to Roz's display.

"You're wearing the diamond necklace!" she exclaims.

"Yes, it's my time of the month," Roz quips.

"I had to come see it up close. It's darling with your outfit. I'll never forget when you wore it the first time. I'd never seen anyone wear jewelry like that at a farmer's market. The next week, I wore my double-strand pearls. You inspired me. You're a pioneer."

ROZ LIKES TO HEAR those words. She comes from a family of pioneers and has considered herself one for a long time.

In the 1850s, her great-grandparents left Ireland during the potato famine to become two of the first Anglo farmers in Ventura County. At its peak, the family amassed five thousand acres. Today, Roz's immediate family—one of the last farming segments of the McGrath clan—organically farms some three hundred acres.

Roz can claim many firsts. She was firstborn in a family of ten. With her mother's recent death, that makes her the matriarch of a family of thirty-three. Roz joined the Na-

tional Organization for Women in its early years and subscribed to *Ms.* the first year the magazine hit the stands.

A former chapter president of the California Women for
Agriculture, she was the first woman to serve on the Ventura County Farm Bureau. She worked on a pilot program in
Ventura to hire women in nontraditional areas like the oil
fields. In 1976, she became the first executive director of
the county's Coalition to End Family Violence. There she
established the first shelter for victims of domestic abuse.
She was the first among the women of Jewelia to persuade
the others to adopt her particular cause—the coalition—as
its premier fund-raiser.

She ran for state assembly three times, when women
comprised less than 15 percent of those in elected positions
there.

"I RAN FOR OFFICE BECAUSE, as a teacher, I was angry that
the State of California, if it were a nation, was the seventh
wealthiest economy on the planet, but in funding for public
education, it was forty-eighth in the country. The experience was disillusioning. Men still dominate politics, and
politics are still corrupt. My second campaign, I ran against
a far-right evangelical, who put flyers all over churches por-
traying me as a pro-choice heathen. That he used churches
as a forum for politics appalled me. I was very naive.

"I was devastated when I lost, because the tally was so
close. I lost by less than half of one percent of the vote. The
hardest part was losing to such a loser, who was backed by
the NRA and the Christian Coalition. Plus, he had far less
experience than I had. I cried for two weeks. I was so grief-

stricken that I had to see a therapist. Then I went back to teaching kindergarten and was fine. I'm glad I ran. I met some incredible people who are friends today. I like to think I inspired other women to run for office.

"What made me much sadder was Bush's selection in Florida in 2000. I felt an overwhelming sense of doom. After 9/11 I wanted to leave the country, move to Ireland, but I was entrenched here. By the time Bush was elected for a second term, I was one depressed Democrat. The group got me over my despair about the election.

"I'm not involved in politics anymore, though if there were a way I could be involved in the impeachment of George Bush I'd be there one hundred percent. I have some 'impeachmints' I keep with me in the car. I thought I'd offer them to the group at the next meeting, get a reaction."

She smiles her knowing smile.

PIONEERS THINK AHEAD, so the first time that Roz hosted the group, she set up a meeting at Ventura's Community Foundation. If the group ever made money, she told the women, they could leave a named legacy to better women's lives.

The second year, she wanted the group to think about women's lives in a different way. The women positioned chairs in a makeshift circle, with Roz seated where she could see everyone. Roz had led classrooms, women's groups, and board meetings for years, so leading tonight's meeting was a natural for her. She was assured and calm and soft-spoken as she went through the business agenda. She didn't hand out her "impeachmints" after all. Instead, like the teacher she was for thirty years, she passed out a writing exercise: "Name a woman of historical significance, living or dead, who you admire. Why do you admire her? How did she have an impact on your life? Do you think the younger generation knows who she is?

"Find a quiet place to write," Roz instructed the women. "You can move to anywhere in the house. Take your time." As the women scattered off to their corners, she smiled. Now this was fun: another class to teach.

The women spent so much time on their answers that by the time they gave them to Roz, it was also time to go home. Later, Roz had more fun guessing the women by their choices. The papers were mostly unsigned, but the writers were easy to discern. Jonell was the only woman who could have selected the anarchist Emma Goldman "because anarchy seems like the most positive affirmation of equality and inclusion." Gunslinging biker babe Mary Osborn chose the risk-taking aviator Amelia Earhart, who ventured into the world of men. Tina Osborne, the Catholic teacher raised near Hollywood, split her vote between Mother Teresa and Jackie Kennedy. Francophile and gourmet Dale Muegenburg chose Julia Child. Nancy Huff chose Condoleezza Rice "because she stands by her commitment to Bush," while Dr. Roz Warner chose Hillary Clinton for "her spectacular health-care initiative." Roz McGrath's choice: birth control activist Margaret Sanger, who was "morally responsible for the betterment of all womankind."

ROZ LIVES IN a charming farmhouse, set high on a hill surrounded by strawberry and raspberry fields. Eucalyptus and avocado trees line the driveway. Magnolia blossoms and sage bushes scent the air. A goldfish pond leads to the front door. A Great White Pyrenees, a Jack Russell terrier, a Welsh corgi, and a beagle move from room to room to patio, their steps a veritable percussion section. The spacious one-story house, with a sweeping view of the Oxnard Plain, exudes both luxury and comfort: a big country kitchen, beamed ceilings, a Celtic harp in front of a brick fireplace, Indian rugs, and books and photos everywhere. Twenty years ago, she bought out her siblings to live in the house in which they'd all grown up.

"This group of women is a strange group for a feminist to belong to," Roz says days after the meeting. "Diamonds are not a feminist thing to own. Books are a feminist thing to own. I have a huge feminist library. My first time with the necklace I didn't know what to do with it. I forgot I had it on. I buy my clothes at Target. The idea of a diamond necklace is absurd to me. It's something Marilyn Monroe wore in a movie. But as a fund-raising tool, that was different. From the start, I could see beyond the wearing of it.

"I don't think most of the women in the group would call themselves feminists. It's not strange as much as disappointing. In the seventies we were on different paths. They were having babies while was I getting an M.A.

"My parents instilled in me the value of education, how it affects your destiny. I was a good student but I flunked ethics in college. The midterm asked us to explain why abortion and homosexuality were morally wrong. I wrote, 'I can't, Father, can you?' I received an automatic F. So much

for a Catholic education. I thought Christians were supposed to teach tolerance.

"I was a hippie but not a dropout. I was an alternative
thinker. I got my politics from my English mother. As a
British citizen, she questioned the American viewpoint on
everything from guns to the environment. She was much
more liberal than her American friends.

"After college I didn't want to be some man's helpmate.
I felt I had a bigger destiny. I went to graduate school in the
Bay Area and specialized in nonsexist education. That's
when I became a feminist. Northern California and Southern California are like two different states. Women here
don't remember what the ERA was. Feminism is still a
threatening word, which saddens me because we all support feminist causes.

"I think education is the key to life. My regret is that I
didn't pursue a Ph.D. in women's studies. It wasn't available
then, and I wouldn't do it now. A Ph.D. would absorb my
life, and I want to garden and write and paint and play my
harp and romp with my dogs. I volunteered with the Red
Cross after Katrina—that's what I'm supposed to be doing
now. I've worked my entire adult life, and I don't ever want
to work full-time again. Plus, a Ph.D. wouldn't make me
feel better about myself. What would do that is writing or
painting something that I could leave behind.

"I knew fairly early in my twenties that I didn't want or
need children to fulfill my life. Parenting is a full-time job
and there's no turning back. I observed my parents dealing
with the demands of ten children. I saw my mother suffer

from constant worry. I knew I wanted something different. This decision has probably had the greatest impact on my life. It's allowed me more time, energy, and money to give to the common good. I have no regrets. I've always had children in my life—students, nieces, nephews, godchildren, children of friends. Nurturing is an important aspect of anyone's well-being, and I like to think I'll be remembered as a nurturing person.

"I've always believed in taking the road less traveled. That's why I said yes to the necklace—it was the road less traveled.

"Even though as a group we come from different places culturally, socially, and politically, as women we can come together to reach for common goals. I've learned that it doesn't matter if we're Republican or Democrat, Catholic or born-again, our goals as women are similar: to raise money for causes that will effect change in our community, that will benefit the lives of others.

"We're the product of our upbringings, which were the most liberating for girls in the history of humankind. We now have the opportunity to use our gifts and to do some good. There's always power in numbers, and this time thirteen proved to be a lucky one."

CHAPTER FOURTEEN

The Experiment

...

Creating its own history

M
. . .

AGGIE HOOD HAD SLEPT ONLY SIX HOURS, BUT SHE awakened eager to start the women's first all-day retreat. She'd made progress with the group. She'd called Jonell and Priscilla to have lunch. When Maggie'd offered to start the retreat with a meditation, the women had agreed. Services at her metaphysical church always started with a centering meditation, which Maggie loved. She opened her fitness classes the same way.

Last night, she'd worked three hours to prepare. She'd written out every word. She'd chosen her music carefully. She'd rehearsed aloud. The contention over "sharing" hadn't been that long ago, so she wanted her meditation to be healing. She knew she'd been given an opportunity, which she didn't want to blow. She didn't want some word slipping out that might offend. She called Patti's older sister, Kathleen, for advice.

Kathleen Morris, a life coach in Ventura, had been volunteering her considerable talents to the group because she loved her sister, had known Jonell for years, and thrilled to any endeavor that contained the word *possibility*. She'd accompanied Jonell the day she purchased the necklace, written name tags and collected donations at the group's fund-raisers, helped with Priscilla's wedding, and coached Jonell before meetings. She'd been so giving and wise that the women named her an "honorary Jewelia."

Kathleen had short gray hair and an open face. Like Patti, she smiled easily and often and, like Patti, when she smiled her hazel eyes glistened.

The women asked Kathleen to lead their retreat, which they wanted to be a conversation for the future and about the future.

In the clubhouse room of her condo complex, Kathleen arranged the black metal chairs in a semicircle, while Patti accessorized the room with white and fuchsia lilies, lavender peonies, and, for calming, lavender diffusers. The sisters set out coffee and juice and fresh fruit.

At eight-fifty A.M., the women started arriving with muffins and cookies. Farmer McGrath toted a bowl of just-picked strawberries from her farm. Along with these offerings of food, the women bore their high spirits like nectar.

Shortly after nine, Maggie inserted *Gentle Landscapes* in her portable CD player. Wearing black workout clothes, she sat up front in Kathleen's director's chair, its cloth back and seat batiked exotically. Maggie was nervous about remembering the words, but she was excited. She loved guiding meditations. She loosened her arms and hands by stretching, then gracefully extended them to rest on her knees in the seated yoga position. Her muscles relaxed. With Indian flutes and woodwinds playing softly in the background, she began:

"I invite you to close your eyes, take a deep breath, recognize we are in the presence of Spirit, of an abundance of love, peace, harmony, and commitment. . . . We come here in a safe place to be fully self-expressed. . . . We bring acceptance, connection, and, most of all, love. . . . We are here today to accomplish something that is bigger than each of us as individuals.

"Imagine sitting on the bank of a river. . . ."

Slowly, carefully, Maggie guided the women to a place free of distraction or discomfort, judgment or criticism. Nancy fidgeted in her chair. Priscilla reached into her purse for her rosary. After fifteen minutes, Maggie brought the meditation to a close:

"Now look into the water to see the reflection of every woman in the group and see reflected back to you love and wisdom and generosity. We release everything that does not serve the higher good. Standing at the water's edge feeling light and free, we await on the threshold of a future and a dream. When you open your eyes, look at the other women's faces. See there compassion and connection. As things unfold, we support each other with love, and so it is. . . ."

Maggie opened her eyes. The room held utter stillness. She'd never heard the group quiet before.

"That was beautiful, Maggie," said Jonell. The others followed with choruses of "That was great," "Yes," "Thank you."

Maggie smiled. Her skin glowed, this time from an inner workout. The women's faces told her that she'd said the right words. She'd been heard.

"What we're about is causing a future," said Kathleen. "So here's the question: What will it take to have this group work for you?"

One by one the women spoke: Active listening. Collective vision. Communication. Gentleness. Respect. Trust.

The morning's discussion focused on "workability"; the afternoon's, on the women's visions for the future.

As each woman had her say, their differences emerged, as though highlighted in boldface. Jonell looked around the room at what she'd created, feeling by turns surprised, hopeful, heartened, and frustrated.

SHE'D STARTED A group of what she'd hoped would be like-minded women only to discover that each woman had her own reason for buying the necklace, and each woman's reason wasn't her reason. Jonell wasn't looking for friends or support or sisterhood. She'd attracted women friends all her life—she owned fourteen bridesmaids' dresses to prove it. For her, the experiment was political, a way to espouse her views on consumption and materialism and the planet's dwindling resources. From the outset, she'd seen the necklace as a vehicle to put her utopian principles into action.

Jonell wasn't looking to change her vision. She was looking to change everyone else's.

Her experiment did change the women, just not the way she'd anticipated.

She wanted the group to raise its consciousness, read more books. Some said, flat-out, *No.*

She wanted the group to walk in peace marches. The Republicans bristled, said, *No way, no how, no.*

She wanted the group to support feminist causes. Some said, *No, other causes too.*

She wanted the group to think globally. Some said, *No, home first.*

She imagined an offbeat social experiment. She hadn't figured on the diversity of the women. She hadn't envisioned the friction.

The friction, however, was key. The conflicts were the very thing that provoked the women to think about who they were and what their lives were about. The controversies pushed them to define their own values more clearly, to take a stand, speak up for what they would and would not support. The group became a mirror to who they were and, perhaps, to who they wanted to be.

Some softened their loud voices; some strengthened their soft voices. Some found their voices for the first time. In this safe community of women, each voice grew more authentic.

Jonell had a strong, authentic voice to begin with, and she never struggles to express her opinions. She displays them, literally, on her clothes, her refrigerator, the walls of her garage. One of her favorites: Tom Robbins's "Flapping your arms can be flying." Rarely is her conversation without a platform nor her enthusiasms disconnected from politics. What she's struggling with now, though paradoxically enjoying at the same time, is expressing her views to women who have become stronger in debating her. Every charismatic leader needs followers, but the women of Jewelia are no longer content to follow.

In spite of herself, Jonell changed too. She learned what all strong people inevitably have to learn, that they have limits. In recognizing hers, she realized a new strength: an ability to let go. To keep her vision intact, to keep the group together, she learned the necessity of compromise. She learned that she could bend. She understands more fully now another of her favorite sayings: "Don't believe everything you think."

Jonell hasn't toned down her voice—she still champions her causes to the group—but she's redirecting it. She hopes to write a column for the Ventura city magazine called "The Champagne Socialist."

"Rather than push a reading list on a group that doesn't want a book club," she says, "maybe I should go where people want to study." Jonell's wide-ranging curiosities have led her to consider graduate programs in urban planning, politics, and gerontology, as well as courses in architecture, archetypes, poetry, and philosophy. In a typical week, Jonell might attend a theosophy lecture, an erotic poetry reading, and a meeting of the city's Downtown Organization. She discusses ideas she's gleaned from the stack of nonfiction tomes and novels at her bedside. She watches *Charlie Rose* every night. Her mind never stops racing, never stops making connections.

"I'd like a job in community activism," she says. "I know I have another career in me. Seeing how receptive other women have been to this experiment, how the town has embraced it, makes me feel that I can do anything."

JONELL IS DRIVING to check out a six-million-dollar estate on Saddle Peak Road in Malibu. The listing sheet advertises a thirteen-acre mountaintop site with a long, gated private drive leading to a modern villa and panoramic views of the city. Jonell loves to drive, and as she steers her seven-year-old silver Mercedes through the winding canyons, she never stops talking. She's frugal by nature, she says, with little furniture or art in her home that didn't come from her mother. But she bought herself a "nice" car because she has to drive clients to "nice" sites. Her son calls her "the only revolutionary who drives a Mercedes."

Jonell's wearing sage-colored soft corduroy pants and a coordinating loose sweater from J. Jill. Her clothes are classic and low-key; her conversation, provocative and high-spirited.

Jonell talks about her fifteen-year marriage. For the last decade, she and her husband have lived in separate houses and enjoyed trysts on weekends. "Living apart gives us all the advantages of an intimate relationship—the familiarity, the safe sex, a date when you need one—without the daily tensions of domestic life," she says. "It keeps the romance and the conversation alive. It's nice to have a man in my life, but I don't need one all the time." She smiles impishly. "Kind of like a diamond necklace."

She talks about her daughter, who's moving out of her mother's house. The transition means that Jonell will be alone for the first time in twenty-eight years. "Who am I going to talk to?" she asks. She laughs after she says this, but concern lurks behind the laughter.

The directions to the remote listing site are vague, but Jonell stays calm as she gets lost twice and maneuvers hairpin turns for an hour on a twisty two-lane road through steep canyons. When she finally arrives at the Malibu mansion, she moves her wiry frame quickly through the rooms, then asks the listing agent half a dozen questions. Fifteen minutes later, she's heading back to Ventura.

An hour later, she stops at the east end of town. There she and her mother own a small trailer park, four small houses on the property, and a liquor and grocery store on the corner. Jonell's late father was an entrepreneur, who in 1964 cannily opened a liquor store near the oil fields teeming with industry.

Jonell's there as landlady collecting rent.

"Hi, Bob. How are ya?"

"Good."

"How do you like the way we painted that trailer? We're going to paint that one over there next."

"One day you may turn this all into a commune," says Bob.

"It already is one," she answers.

Jonell walks quickly but stops to chat with everyone she sees.

"Hi, Charlie, how ya doing? Have you got your patch on?"

An elderly man sitting in a lawn chair rolls up his sleeve to show her his nicotine patch.

"I've been smoking sixty-five years, started at fifteen," he says. "And now I've quit."

"That's so great, Charlie. That's marvelous. I'm proud of you. Keep up the good work."

The corrugated metal trailers with the ceramic frogs and plastic flamingos on the lawn are a far cry from the Southern California mansions, but Jonell is as comfortably at home here as she is in Malibu.

Since working in real estate, she says, she's thought a lot about housing and what home ownership looks like when you don't need a single-family home anymore. She often fantasizes with some of the other women in Jewelia about how they'll live together one day in the trailer park— extensively renovated, of course. In the fantasy they'll share one large-screen TV, one hot tub, one garden. "I en-vision it with both men and women," she says, "but more women respond to the idea. Why should we move to some assisted living facility with strangers when we can live with our friends?

"Jewelia is turning out to be a dry run for living together. If we can share a necklace, we can share real estate.

"Ownership is overrated. We should elevate sharing. Wealth is individual; sharing is collective. We are not what we own. We are what we do, who we help, and the difference we make in the world. At the beginning, the group was so narrow in its concept of sharing. We think that by sharing we give up something, that we get less. But the more we've shared the necklace, the more profound the experience has become. By sharing, we've gotten so much more. If we share, there's enough on the planet for everyone."

"Sharing really is the way to happiness."

THE WOMEN OF JEWELIA came together as friends, acquain-tances, or strangers. They evolved into family. Like all fam-ilies, their distinctive personalities rub up against one another, producing dysfunctional moments.

Nevertheless, the group is cohesive, invested not just in a blingy necklace but also in each other's lives. In the past three years, the women have come to know and care for one another's families. Daily e-mails relay their children's successes, their mothers' hospitalizations, their grandchildren's christenings or mitzvahs. Through cyberspace, they share jokes and inspirational stories, pleas and prayers. They ask Dr. Roz for medical advice and Jone for design ideas. The constant e-mail chatter—what lured Priscilla to her first meeting—holds them enmeshed in one another's lives, helps them push past their different approaches to life, and stretches their tolerance.

They know they'll survive as friends. They don't know how they'll evolve as a group. They couldn't have predicted what's happened. They're hoping for more surprises. Jonell envisions an intergenerational group, double in size, wider in reach. She thinks that, largely due to Patti, they can be an even greater force in the community. "Jewelia has led us to boldness," she says. "As a group, we're so much more powerful than we are as individuals."

Among their most recent philanthropies, the group has adopted Gale Levesque, a fifty-two-year-old homeless woman who desperately wanted a job. The women bought her a cell phone with six months of minutes, bus passes good for two months, and two weeks at the Ocean View Motel. Jonell helped her compose a résumé and drove her to her first interview. Gale landed the part-time job and is looking for another one. She calls herself "the fourteenth sister."

This past Christmas, the women of Jewelia discovered that the Salvation Army's local Transitional Living Center had an empty kitchen. Gourmet chef Dale asked the center for a wish list, and the group filled the cabinets with commercial pots and pans, small appliances and cooking utensils. A plaque inscribed "Jewelia's Kitchen" commemorates the necklace's namesake. Patti's continually on the lookout for new places in town in need. "Jewelia's made me more aware of what I have and what others don't have," she says. "Now I see the difference between spending five hundred dollars on a purse and feeding the homeless."

TODAY, THE NECKLACE itself is rarely part of the women's conversation. But it continues to be a part of other people's. As word has gotten around, the necklace has taken on a life and itinerary of its own.

Albert Garibay, fifty-seven, a retired deputy with Ventura's sheriff's department, needed a gift idea for his daughter Jenny's twenty-ninth birthday. She'd been so wonderful helping him take care of his elderly mother that he wanted to do something special for her. What could he think of that would show the depth of his appreciation? A CD? She already had a stack of them. A blouse? Even he knew that was too ordinary. He'd seen Jenny pore over catalogs from Tiffany's looking at jewelry she couldn't afford. He'd heard her talk about the Ventura diamond necklace. He'd seen her stare at it at the Van Gundy wedding. She'd followed the necklace's history by reading every word written about it. She'd never think that such a piece of jewelry would be possible for her, thought Albert, but he could imagine what she couldn't, and what he could imagine, he could make real.

He called Priscilla Van Gundy, a longtime friend who'd

been both a grade school classmate and a co-worker at the county jail. "I need a favor," he said.

At nine A.M. the morning of Jenny's birthday, Albert, his wife, his mother, and Priscilla and Tom Van Gundy surprised Jenny at the medical office where she worked as an assistant. "Happy Birthday from Jewelia," said Priscilla as she laced Jenny's neck with the diamonds. "She's yours today."

Jenny burst into tears. Then Albert cried, too. He knew he'd found the perfect gift.

Six months later, Jenny still raves about her birthday present. "I know it was only a piece of jewelry," she says, "but with it my parents gave me a once-in-a-lifetime experience."

ACROSS THE COUNTRY, in Cudjoe Key, twenty miles north of Key West, Judi Gibbs had called her neighbor Mary O'Connor every time Mary came to town. "Do you have the necklace?" Judi would ask. The two women's Florida visits often overlapped but not when Mary was wearing the necklace. Finally, after two and a half years, Mary O'Connor called her friend and neighbor. "I've got the necklace," she said, "and some of the women, too."

Judi Gibbs, fifty-nine, a retired accounting professor, was so excited that she immediately called her women's group, the Divine Divas, to come to her home to meet the Ventura women and see their diamond necklace up close. Four hours later, nine Divas greeted five women of Jewelia. Within seconds of walking in the house, Mary unclasped the diamonds from around her neck.

"What are you doing?" Judi asked.

"I'm taking it off so you can wear it," Mary answered, transferring the necklace to Judi.

"Oh my gosh!" Judi exclaimed, literally jumping, racing to the mirror, jumping again. "Oh my gosh!"

Judi turned to Mary. "I thought you'd just bring it in a jewelry box and we'd look at it. I never imagined I'd get to wear it!" She ran to the mirror again. "I've got to change my clothes!"

Judi ran to her bedroom to trade her collared, long-sleeved white cotton shirt for a low-cut tank top. "Oh my gosh!' she said again and again, running back to the mirror, her smile as wide as Carol Channing's, whom she resembled. While Judi was prancing around the room, the Divas, ranging in age from fifty to eighty-two, besieged the Ventura women with questions: How does the sharing work? How do you raise money? Can we start a charter group?

IN THE END, a diamond necklace did make a statement, not about wealth and status, but about the needs that cross cultures and link generations, the connections that transcend time and place. There may be no escaping our material culture, but thirteen women in Ventura, California, showed that we can reframe it on our terms.

The women of Jewelia transformed a symbol of privilege into an experiment in humanity. In so doing, they rewrote the narrative of desire.

ACKNOWLEDGMENTS

...

Thanks to agents David Kuhn and Lisa Bankoff for creating the collaboration; editor Susan Mercandetti for envisioning the story's structure; the people of Ventura County for generously giving their time to be interviewed; Michael Parrish for providing invaluable counsel; Jane Ferry for offering honest feedback and support; Dina Pielaet for taking such wonderful photographs; Martha Baker for editing with insight and flair; and Abigail Plesser for delightfully shepherding the manuscript through production.

CHERYL JARVIS is a journalist and essayist and the author of *The Marriage Sabbatical: The Journey That Brings You Home*. Her byline has appeared in numerous publications, including *The Wall Street Journal*, the *Chicago Tribune*, *Cosmopolitan*, *Redbook*, and *Reader's Digest*. A former television producer and magazine and newspaper editor, she has taught writing at the University of Southern California and at Washington University and Webster University in St. Louis.

The text of this book was set in Filosofia. It was designed in 1996 by Zuzana Licko, who created it for digital typesetting as an interpretation of the sixteenth-century typeface Bodoni. Filosofia, an example of Licko's unusual font designs, has classical proportions with a strong vertical feeling, softened by rounded droplike serifs. She has designed many typefaces and is the cofounder of *Emigre* magazine, where many of them first appeared. Born in Bratislava, Czechoslovakia, Licko came to the United States in 1968. She studied graphic communications at the University of California, Berkeley, graduating in 1984.